THE
TALKING DEAD

A

COLLECTION

OF

MESSAGES

FROM

BEYOND THE VEIL,

1850s to 1920s.

Edited by Marc Hartzman

New York

Published by Curious Publications
101 W. 23rd St. #318
New York, NY 10011
curiouspublications.com

Book introduction and selection introduction text
copyright © 2020 by Marc Hartzman.

Cover design elements are from *Ghost Land, or Researches Into the Mysteries if Occultism*, by Emma Hardinge Britten. Chicago: Progressive Thinker Publishing House, 1905.

Back cover illustration from *The Encyclopaedia of Death and Life in the Spirit-World*, by J. R. Francis. Chicago: The Progressive Thinker Publishing House, 1903.

Frontispiece from the collection of Marc Hartzman.

Automatic writing image preceding the bibliography from *Psychography: A Treatise on One of the Objective Forms of Psychic or Spiritual Phenomena*, by "M. A. (Oxon)". London: W. H. Harrison, 1878.

ISBN-13: 978-0-9862393-8-0

Printed and bound in the United States of America.

For the living.

CONTENTS

Introduction   11

Spirit Teachings

Spirit World and Spirit Life   19
    The Spirit Body   20
    Negative Aspect of Spirit Life   24
    On Visions   27
    On the Unjust Accumulation of Wealth   28
    A Few Notes on Evil   31

Letters from a Living Dead Man   33
    The Wand of Will   34
    A Light Behind the Veil   35
    Don't Forget to Hydrate   35
    Individual Hells   36
    The Game of Make-Believe   36
    The Leisure of the Soul   38
    An Unexpected Warning   41

Psychography: Marvelous Manifestations of Psychic Power
  Given Through the Mediumship of Fred P. Evans   45
    A Slate of Many Languages   47

The Encyclopaedia of Death and Life in the Spirit World   51
    Death Considered by Spirit Lucretus   52

Automatic or Spirit Writing With Other Psychic Experiences   61
    A Q&A on the Nature of Death   62
    Spirit World FAQs   62

After Death, or Letters from Julia and *The Blue Island:*
Experiences of a New Arrival Beyond the Veil   71

Return to Friends	73
The Life Beyond	73
The Nothingness of Things	73
Wanted, A Bureau of Communication	74
The Dangers of Communicating Across the Border	74
The Same Yet Not the Same	75
A Flight Through Space	76
Chapter 1: The Arrival	78
Chapter 2: The Blue Island	81
Chapter 3: Interesting Buildings	84
Chapter 4: Life on the Island	86
The Next World Interviewed	91
Prof. Agassiz on Evolution	92
Herodotus Discusses a Pre-Historic Race of Man	95
Pheneas Speaks	99
"The Greatest Thing That Could Possibly Happen for Humanity"	100
"The Rubbish Heap of Humanity"	100
"Surely I Could Not Have Liked That"	101
"Humanity Will Be Staggered"	102
"We Do Not Eat Meat"	102
"Be On Your Guard"	103

Afterlifestyles of the Rich and Famous

Abraham Lincoln	109
My Passage to Spirit-Life	110
A World War I Warning	113
An Interview	115
George Washington	117
Experiences and Opinions	119
On Government	128
"Forget Your Pompous Pride"	129

Edgar Allan Poe	131
The Dark World Described	132
The Lost Soul	133
An Untitled Poem	134
Spirit Poem on the Raven	137
William Shakespeare	143
Hamlet in Heaven	146
Sonnets of Shakespeare's Ghost	157
An Interview	159
Mark Twain	163
A Chat with Mark Twain	164
Jap Herron	171
Benjamin Franklin	180
Aphorisms from the Afterlife	179
On Invention	184
On Liberty	186
Peter Cooper	199
Educational Institutions in the Spirit-World	200
Prince Albert	203
England and the Queen	204
Emanuel Swedenborg	209
Magnetism and Communication	210
A Self-Retraction	212

Heaven on Mars

Description of the Journey to Mars, and Wonderful Information Furnished by Madam Ehrenborg	219
Bibliography	257

INTRODUCTION

IF THE DEAD could talk, what would they say? What wondrous things would we learn? During the height of Spiritualism in the late nineteenth and early twentieth century, mediums claimed to have found out.

These voices from beyond began in 1848, when Maggie and Kate Fox (fourteen and ten years old, respectively) heard rapping noises on walls and furniture from inside their Hydesville, New York, home. They claimed to be communicating with the spirit of a man who'd died there. The Fox's story spread, they took their talents on tour, and a new religion, Spiritualism, was born.

The sister act was quickly followed by a brother act, Ira and William Davenport. The young innovative showmen developed a "spirit cabinet" that seemed to conjure up instrument-playing ghosts. Ira and William would invite audience members to tie them to benches inside the cabinet, have the doors closed, and then summon the spirits. Guitars, banjos, and other clanging instruments would then be seen flying around through a small window and heard making a cacophony of noise.

While the Davenports brought music to the spirit show, another medium expanded the creative possibilities by channeling ghosts through painting. British Spiritualist Georgiana Houghton began producing artwork from the afterlife in 1859 when spirits coursing through her during séances would create drawings and watercolors.

Another early act who caused great wonder and excitement was a Scottish-born medium named Daniel Dunglas (D. D.) Home. In the early 1850s he began touring America and Europe, hobnobbing with kings, queens and the wealthy while holding séances and occasionally levitating. He was known to have floated out of a window high off the ground then float back into the home through another window. So unusual were Home's skills that he was nicknamed the Napoleon of

Necromancy and the Past Grand Master of Mediums.

Spiritualism evangelist and Sherlock Holmes creator, Sir Arthur Conan Doyle, spoke highly of Home in his 1918 book, *The New Revelation*, calling him "the greatest medium of all," and noting that he "showed his phenomena in broad daylight, and was ready to submit to every test and no charge of trickery was ever substantiated against him."

By the late 1870s there were more than eleven million Americans identifying as Spiritualists and tens of thousands of mediums preaching the good word of the dead.

The dead, as it turned out, had a lot to say. They used Ouija boards or took control of mediums' hands through a process called psychography, or automatic writing, to speak their minds.

Doyle spoke highly of many of these psychic wonders, too, convinced that contact with the dead was possible. He had attended his first séance in 1880 and afterward proclaimed, "After weighing the evidence, I could no more doubt the existence of the phenomena than I could doubt the existence of lions in Africa."

But his steadfast belief in spirits didn't come till decades later, when he believed he heard a personal message from his son, Kingsley, who had died in a World War I battle. Doyle's wife, Jean, soon claimed to have developed her own psychic powers and began channeling ghosts. By this time, Doyle and Harry Houdini had begun a friendship, though the magician did not share in the author's Spiritualist beliefs. This, naturally, put a bit of a strain of their relationship.

In 1922, Doyle invited the master of escape to a sitting with Jean in an Atlantic City hotel room. There, she planned to channel Houdini's mother and produce a message through automatic writing. By the end of the séance, she'd scribbled fifteen pages of notes from the magician's mother. But Houdini wasn't buying it. After all, his mother's English was terrible—she couldn't have possibly said any of what was written.

Houdini, in fact, wasn't buying any messages from any medium and spent years exposing their tricks. Meanwhile Doyle continued believing and preaching their powers through lectures and books. One book, *The Coming of Fairies*, even announced the existence of tiny fairytale-like creatures and included photos. Years later the teenage girls who'd taken the fairy images admitted they were a hoax.

Their confession came long after the Fox sisters, who, toward the end of the nineteenth century, explained their rapping act through an ability to crack their toe joints.

Still, people wanted to believe, no matter how much people like Houdini exposed fraudulent mediums.

Oftentimes the messages received from these spirits were religious in nature, promoting moral and philosophical beliefs. Even when they came from celebrity spirits like Edgar Allan Poe and William Shakespeare, who weren't about to let a little thing like death stop their prolific writing. And as you'll read in the final section of this collection, the dead even spoke about Mars—in great detail.

The selections in this book have been pulled from a variety of Spiritualist publications dating back as early as the 1850s and as late as the early 1920s. I've offered brief context with each section before presenting the alleged words from beyond the veil, as they originally appeared (including the occasional antiquated spellings and hyphenations).

If you choose to believe the dead can indeed communicate with us, then perhaps these words will offer the peace and comfort I believe most mediums wished them to do. If not, enjoy these messages for the entertainment value they offer, and the sense of wonder they invoke today, knowing that at one point, more than a hundred years ago, so many people felt certain that the dead could talk.

— MARC HARTZMAN

SPIRIT TEACHINGS

Thanks to mediums across the country, the mystery of death no longer had to be a mystery. The messages they claimed to have received offered answers to age-old questions about the afterlife and what we the living can expect when our bodies expire. Where do our spirits go? What keeps us busy when we're dead? Will we need to eat and drink? These experiences and observations often seemed to confirm what religious leaders had been preaching for years about the greatness of God and living an ethical life. If one questioned religious beliefs before, how could they question messages from the infinite wisdom of the dead?

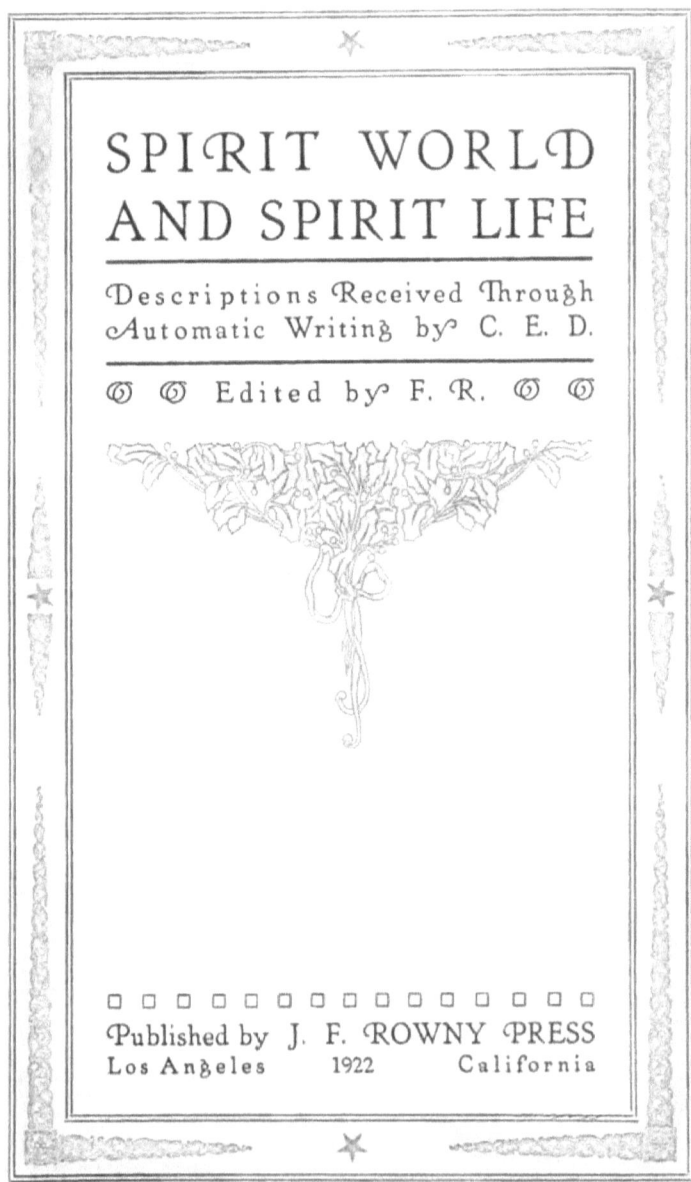

SPIRIT WORLD AND SPIRIT LIFE

In 1922's Spirit World and Spirit Life, *Fred Rafferty wrote messages he claimed came from his sister Dee, who had died months earlier. She was joined by a spirit named Mary Bosworth, described as "the good angel who was sent to meet her as she passed into the Beyond." The following pages offer descriptions of the spirit world, as revealed in several conversations from Rafferty's writings.*

THE SPIRIT BODY

IT is difficult for the human mind to realize any conditions that lie outside the five physical senses. These, since man was created, have been his guide and protection until he can scarcely conceive of intelligent life existing without them. The spirit body, which cannot be tested through these senses,—sight without eyes, hearing without ears, thought without brain, touch, movement, all without the physical equipment,—is nearly if not quite incomprehensible. Our repeated questions have brought answers which have enlightened our dull comprehension to a certain extent. We asked one evening if the statement was true that spirit bodies were etheric.

"It is true that our bodies are etheric in substance; and we admire more and more their adaptation to spiritual environment. We do not have the material senses, or the material substance; we are constructed, so far as the body is concerned, of finer material. We are not conscious of our bodies, for they serve us without pain or weariness, and we are not constantly taking care of them as on earth."

'Can you see each other?'

"We can see each other, but perceive through different senses. You need not fear for the expression of spiritual life or spirit body, for all is far better than any you have imagined."

'You do not breathe; do you have lungs?'

"No, nor any of the other organs necessary for earth life. The material organs were created for man's use during his material life and are quite unnecessary here. We do not need eyes nor ears, for sight and hearing are through spirit powers; yet we have the semblance of these in our spirit forms. We do not need the organs of speech, nor the mouth, nor other organs of the material outfit; yet the outline of the material form is beautiful, and we can well assume that form for ourselves. We have no material limbs; yet when you see us the likeness will not be missing. We love the old familiar form and it becomes more beautiful here, and remains."

'Do you have the sense of touch?'

"We might if we chose, for spirit can give sensation as perfectly as the nerves, but we do not often require this."

One evening Mary wrote:
"Many friends are here, wishing news from earth."
'Are they all in this room?'
"We can get into smaller compass than you imagine; yet if you could see us you would recognize every one."
'What are you, anyway? Just a thought floating around?'
"No! We have forms, and they are very like our earthly ones, only better. Spirit is not confined to any particular length, breadth, or thickness. Nevertheless, we have bodies, and do have size if we wish."

I spoke of reading of debates among monks of olden times over the question of how many angels could stand on a needle's point.

"That is a good question. I know I could balance on a needle's point, or I could occupy as much room as I ever did on earth."

'How did you come into the room? The windows and doors are closed.'

"You need not think that walls are obstacles to us. We pass through them as easily as light passes through glass."

'How does the wall appear to you?'

"Something like a cloud, through which we move as easily as you would walk through a fog."

'You are like an X-ray then?'

"That is a good comparison as far as movement through obstacles is concerned."

'How about rain and storms?'

"All weather is bright to us. Changes in temperature make no difference, nor clouds, nor rain. We could move away from any tornado if we chose, or we could stay in it and enjoy its motion. We could outride any tempest in a flash, and the rain cannot even moisten the texture of our raiment. Can't you understand, you human child? Wait till you come and we will prove to you how superior we are to nature's elements."

'Can you touch each other: shake hands, for instance?'

"What are those motions except to express thought? We do not need such expressions, for with us thought expresses itself without medium of touch or of speech, although we can use these if we wish."

Sis, always doubtful and confused about the powers of spirit, asked:

'With your spirit sight, can you see Dee?'

"She is here and smiling that you are still so ignorant of spirit power. She is near you and could touch you, yet you are doubtful of her presence."

'How does she look?'

"As she looked when on earth, only far more beautiful. Her robes fall about her with soft, cloud-like radiance, and express the same sense of harmony that she loved on earth."

Then Sis asked Dee to tell her how Mary looked.

"Mary has dark eyes and is taller than I am. 'We are not alike in looks, but are alike in perceptions, tastes, and desires. We have different work, and each

has different interests; yet we are closely related. Can you understand?"

'How about her dress?'

"She wears delicate colors, as nearly all do; sometimes rose color, pink, or lavender, but in shades more delicate than any you know. We are never afraid of injuring our robes, for they are not subject to wear or soil. They are never in the way, and we do not step on or get entangled in them.

"We are clothed in garments that correspond to our mental and spiritual condition. You will appear in a simple white garment at first, and this will change as you change. Mental qualities express themselves outwardly, and different minds express different colors. Minds that are filled with doubt are sometimes clothed in incongruous colors. The destructive forces have coarse garments of the most discordant colors. They imagine themselves in gorgeous apparel. But they will sometime see themselves as they are, which will be when they reach out for something better.

"The clothes are made by thought processes, as are all our beautiful surroundings. We are clothed when we first arrive, and only the color remains for us, which is decided by our own thought lives. We can change when we choose, but few changes are made, for the material is indestructible."

We had been talking of dress one evening, and jokingly asked about the prevailing fashions there.

"We could never describe the fashions here, for they change with lightning swiftness. We would have to describe the prevailing thought instead. Thought manifests itself in changes of color. Character always differentiates the appearance. The appearance is lovely in proportion as the spirit is lovely. Dress is more than external adornment; it becomes a sort of symbol of character."

One evening my grandfather came, and Mary said:

"He is very bright and happy looking, and if you could see his perfect form and youthful appearance, you would not be calling him grandfather."

I spoke of his stooping shoulders when on earth, and Mary came back with this:

"Must I repeat, that no physical imperfection appears in the spirit form? He is not surprised that you remember his bent figure, but thinks he will be able to surprise you when you come."

A young soldier of whom we had known, had been blown to atoms by a shell. We asked if that would interfere with the spirit's entrance into that life.

"The body does not imprison the spirit; neither can the spirit be injured. The soul of the young soldier would arrive here as perfectly as if borne on angel wings."

'Then spirit is not subject to accidents?'

"Spirit is superior to all conditions. I could meet lightning without sensation, or ride on the wings of a tornado, or drop into the greatest heat, or move among polar snows, and all sensations would be pleasant. Spirit is the controlling power. I do not quite know how to express it, but spirit is above and beyond any conflict of the elements, or any material conditions. In our movement through the ether, we have no sense of obstruction, and we pass easily through matter that you consider solid. We are infinitely finer than any material known on earth."

'Could you descend into the earth?'

"It is through spirit that the treasures of the earth have been found. It is through spiritual impressions on the mind of man that he has been sent to seeking and using the hidden riches which are there for the finding."

Speaking of the higher planes, we are told:

"Life on the higher planes is more ethereal than here, and all conditions are more ethereal. Coming to this plane from a higher one is a little like descending from an altitude where the air is light, to a lowland where the air is dense. Like a life accustomed to the rarefied air of mountain tops, descending into deep pits of the earth, where the air is too heavy for them to breathe."

THE NEGATIVE ASPECT OF SPIRIT LIFE

PROBABLY very few people have really tried to analyze the conditions, and tried to determine what activities and occupations engage the time and attention of the inhabitants of the spirit world. When one realizes that there are no material bodily requirements whatever in the spirit life, and when one really comprehends what a gap would be left in our life here if all such activities were unnecessary, it opens up a whole new field of thought. The subject of what one would not find or need there,—what one might call the negative aspect of spirit life,—was brought up for Mary's comments, and a copy of our record for that evening is here given. Sis and I had talked of it a little, and when I turned to Mary, I said:

'In the first place, you have no day and no night, and no divisions of time.'

"No day and no night and no divisions of time, you say. We have the divisions of work and study and recreation and quiet hours or times for ourselves. Do you not divide your days by actions rather more than you think? There are the meal times, the work times, the play times, and the resting times. That is very similar to our divisions."

'Yes, but you do not reckon time by hours and minutes.'

"Hardly. We have a system or order of work and study, though what you call hours and minutes are not so counted by us. The divisions of time are not arbitrary, but I am thinking how to tell you of the orderly way in which we work. Perhaps if I call it (this by way of illustration) a central office, where the plans of work are arranged and messengers sent to us when we are needed, it may help you a little."

'Well, again: You have no need for food, and so no rivalry in obtaining it; no buying or selling, no business of any kind, no money, no medium of exchange.'

"We are as busy as you. We exchange many things, which might be called barter. For instance: I study something I wish to perfect myself in, and teach, perhaps, my very teacher in some other branch. We exchange many things, sometimes work, sometimes ideas, sometimes the many acts of love or friendliness; but all without your medium of exchange, money. We have love instead, or, if to those we do not know, whatever courtesy suggests. So you see we have a busy trading system, and enjoy it too, and no one becomes bankrupt."

Sis said it was very difficult for her to realize that there would be no desire to eat or sleep.

"You will never miss either. Instead, you will be delighted that the sordid occupations of life do not interfere with your progress."

'So much of life here is made up of chasing the dollar with which to buy food and comfort, it would seem that many people would be completely lost over there. What will a banker do there, for instance?'

"Will you know that his training there will not be lost here. He may not handle money, but there are many other ways in which that trained accuracy will be of service."

'Then, your travel is so different. You have no railroads, no trains, no automobiles, no airplanes, no steamships."

"Wait till you come and we take you on a trip to some far off place. The mode of travel will be as much finer, as your Cadillac is finer than a wheelbarrow!"

'Having no need of the things that money buys, there can be with you no jealousies because of place or position attained by material blessings.'

"They who serve most are the greatest here. There is no computing of place or position except by service or wisdom. Service may be of the intelligence, or of the spiritual gifts, or the more common activities; but the wiser the service, or the more loving and unselfish the giving of one's self:—these are the things that give prominence in spirit life."

'You have no thieves or robbers, and no need for insurance policies.'

"We have the unworthy ones to guide and the wicked ones to

convert, and the time and patience given to this work is more than any occupation on earth would probably demand. The unworthy ones are always with us, therefore that work is never done."

I said they had no color line, therefore no race prejudice; and Sis asked if spirits were always white.

"Not that exactly, but spirit is not black or red or yellow or brown. It is spirit, that is all."

When we read this later, Mary corrected it by saying: "That would seem to make spirit a colorless substance. That would be quite the opposite of the truth. Spirit is white, in a way, because spirit represents truth, beauty, and nobility of character. The character determines the exterior, and purity of soul expresses itself in purity of appearance."

'Then, as you have remarked several times, you have no care of the house or clothing or person.'

"It makes us almost weary to think of all these things; but your list has brought to our attention our freedom and our joys. We become so accustomed to our blessings that we perhaps forget a little, and it is good to be reminded."

'But, Mary, what are the youngsters going to do? There are no games of foot-ball, no baseball, no tennis, no golf, no billiards, no card-playing!'

"Don't you worry. There are pleasures beyond these, and there are delightful occupations that take the time."

Sis spoke of the wonders of mountain scenery here, and asked if any such would be there.

"What did you hear from the college professor in regard to the desires of life here? Were you not to see the rugged and the grand, as well as the quiet beauty of valley and stream? He is right, and there will be no disappointment for you."

'But the snowy mountain ranges here have an attraction just because we cannot easily reach them. Dee could there go in an instant to anything she wanted to see.'

"She would not be impressed in the way you would sense it; but it would impress her, nevertheless. You can look into fathomless space here as well as there. You can see infinite distance, and the evidences of infinite power. And you can see the wonderlands of strange planets."

Sis then spoke of the Spanish dances and the play of color in the 'Mission Play' which we had just seen.

"Will you try to imagine the grace and beauty of motion that is without fatigue, dress fairer than any the world has seen; beauty of person, of dress, of motion, and all without vanity or selfishness? You cannot get beyond earth comparisons, I know; but if your spirit sight could be clear for one minute even, you would never again believe that heaven can lose by comparison with the joys or the beauties of the world."

'Well, we have covered the ground fairly well with the negative illustrations, though no doubt it could be elaborated almost endlessly.'

"We think you are answered in a way; but one half-hour of vision, yes, even one half-minute, would be more convincing."

ON VISIONS

THE Visions which are often times seen by the people on the Earth, both in their waking hours, and in their slumbers, or what you call dreams, are nothing more or less than the manifestations of Spirits from different Spheres. This depends entirely upon what the Vision may be; if it is for a good purpose and for a pure, purpose, then it must necessarily come from those Spirits of greater Spirituality than in the first Sphere, but again these manifestations, or visions may be from the Earth bound Spirits, who want to make themselves known, or perhaps are very desirous of giving to those whom the vision is presented to, such manifestations as shall awaken their interest, that they may investigate farther and then in this manner, the Earth bound Spirits will take their chances in making themselves known, and giving unto such persons their wishes. This is manipulated by the same Electrical forces and Currents as are used by the Guides, for the Mediums in Clairvoyance, Clairaudience, or all other phases of Mediumship, and if the Vision is in the manner of a face, or form that is seen, then this tends to what is called Materialization. This is brought about by these Electrical forces and the drawing of the material magnetism of the person who sees the Vision, and it is as it were, a counterpart of their own physical, but with the soul of the one that is seen shining forth through the face of the semi-physical body, or in other words the elements and material necessary to materialize are drawn from the individual who has the vision.

ON THE UNJUST ACCUMULATION OF WEALTH

IT is a pleasure to me, to have this blessed privilege, of coming back to Earth again, and coming to the people, and appealing to them that there is something higher and something of greater worth in life, and in the Spheres Beyond, than the accumulation of the Earth wealth.

Now in this chapter, I am talking especially to those people, who have been so fortunate that they are enabled to accumulate more of the Earth's wealth than is necessary for their own individual necessities.

Now man and woman of the Earth, and of its wealth, what is your duty to your brother man and sister woman? It is not that you keep on in your life of hoarding your treasures for your own selfish pleasure and gain, and depriving those who, if they but had the actual necessities that they needed in life, they might better awaken to the possibilities of a better life. Are you not in your selfishness in hoarding your wealth responsible in a measure, for a good share of the evil on Earth? Take for instance the idle men of the day, would they be idle if this wealth were more evenly distributed among mankind?

And if in their idleness they are tempted and fall, is it the wealth of the earth plane that reaches down and lifts these fallen men or women and assists them, when the wealth holders are perfectly able to assist, and with out injuring their own earthly prospects in any manner? I say to you, that thou hast it upon thy head, if thou dost not reach out to help those beneath you, when you see that just a little of that which you have accumulated would keep them from this temptation and give to them at least a decent life on earth, and in giving encouragement and a betterment and an incentive for the right life, is it not more to you, O wealthy man, than the hoarding of your treasures on earth, which shall be taken from you as you pass the portals, and will ne'er be counted in your favor as a farthing or a jewel of any price?

It is but a worthless drug upon your shoulders, when you pass to the higher Spheres and then you will be confronted with this; What hast thou done for Mankind? What hast thou done to assist thou brother man? I plead with thee awaken now, to the necessity of giving a part at least of your hoarded treasures to those in need, remember those who are tempted to crime, are oftentimes but the results of your own hoarding and your own neglect of your duty to your fellow men.

When on Earth, I was a public speaker, and I was constantly confronted with this question of what could be done to arouse those who had plenty of the Earth's wealth to reach out and help those who were leading the life that would meet with punishment and darkness in the future. Since my Transition to the Higher Spheres, I have traversed through the first and second and now am in the Third Sphere and I find wherever I have traveled the results O man of wealth of your wrong living, for I have seen what you might have done, and I have seen where you might have assisted others, and I have seen where you yourself, have darkened your own future life in the Spheres in which you will be called to dwell. Now man of the greedy heart, O man of the selfish nature, is it not the time for you to arouse yourself and cast from you that chain that shall bind you down and chain you to the darkened Sphere with the lowest, the murderer and those of the criminal class, for you have sinned as they have sinned, and to me your crime is greater because you are supposed to be of a mind that is capable to rise above the evils of the Earth. As I look upon the results of this uneven and unjust accumulation of wealth, it seems to me from the Spirit side, that I never sensed the evil of the man who lived for the greed of gain as I now do.

I have had my experience with many of those, who allowed the earth messengers or mediums, on earth for the other worlds, suffer in vain for even the necessary dollars to carry them from one place to the other that they might bring the glad tidings of the future life, but I never on Earth comprehended what this all meant until I passed to the Beyond, and again I plead with you O man and woman of wealth, that there is something for you in the life beyond, other than this accumulation of the mighty dollar, which is but a selfish greed within your heart.

That greed not only destroys the best within you, and numbs it, and creates within yourself no intellectual power, and you are hampering those, who should have at least a fair chance to live in some manner of com fort, if not of privileges, that wealthy ones are so ready to accept for themselves.

In my investigations in the first Sphere I found that there are many and numerous Millionaires there, who had supposed that they were the great Lords of Creation, who are to-day down in the very depths of despair and as it were, are at the very foot of the ladder and they have yet to reach out and grasp and climb, as the criminal has, because they too have failed, when it was near them and within their power to assist mankind, and make themselves more spiritual.
On Earth they have grasped and robbed whom they did business with, for their own personal gain, and I find these Millionaires classed with the criminals who have in their ignorance committed crime.

Is this not enough to awaken you, and is this not enough to bring you to the sense of reform, and to stop your reaching out and ever grasping for that which does not properly belong to you, for no man is entitled to more than he can necessarily use for the necessary comforts, and all that he gains then, is of little worth to him, when he passes to the life of the angel world?

Then there is another side to the story, for you have a chance if you but will before the hour of thy transition comes, to redeem your self by letting out this wealth in a manner that shall aid and assist in the enlightenment of mankind. This is a period when it requires a war, a Revolutionary War I might say, to awaken the masses to the realization of the evil that is on this earth plane.

The time is here O man of worth, when you can redeem yourself and commence the life that shall lead you to a home not of bitterness, sorrow and punishment but one of glorious and grand spirituality, that shall make your soul forever in peace, comfort and contentment for all time, if ye will seek for the higher in life, and ye shall find and it will be given unto thee O Man.

A FEW NOTES ON EVIL

Q.—Does evil persist into the higher planes?
A.—No; one leaves all that as one ascends; or, rather, one does not ascend until all evil has been eliminated.

Q.—Can an evil spirit enter into or take possession of a human being?
A.—Every one is free to control his own individuality. We are not allowed to take possession.

Q.—But there are apparent possessions; how about them?
A.—Evil spirits break the laws here just as they do there, but there must be a receptive attitude in the individual or no possession would be possible.

Q.—Then the old story of selling one's self to the devil may be approximately true?
A.—Yes; many have done this unknowingly.

Q.—Can you tell us the origin of evil?
A.—That is not for us to know at present. The origin is so far away in an unknown past that only the Creator of us all can rightly tell of its origin and use. But we know that all things work toward a final greater good, and that is sufficient for us at present.

Q.—Is the percentage of good people any greater now than a hundred years ago?
A.—The percentage is far greater than formerly. But the quiet lives of the good, with their unseen and unselfish service, do not get to the knowledge of the public as do the riotous actions of the evil-minded ones.

Q.—Is the world growing better?
A.—The good are growing better; the evil are growing more evil still.

LETTERS
FROM A
LIVING DEAD MAN

WRITTEN DOWN
BY
ELSA BARKER

WITH AN INTRODUCTION

NEW YORK
E. P. DUTTON & COMPANY
681 FIFTH AVENUE

LETTERS FROM A LIVING DEAD MAN

Elsa Barker claims that she was not a spiritualist, nor was the friend who wrote letters through her hand for eleven months in the early 1900s. The communications first began when she felt compelled to write, picked up a pencil, and found her hand "seized as if from the outside, and a remarkable message of a personal nature came, followed by the signature 'X.'" This "X" turned out to be a friend, a "well-known lawyer nearly seventy years of age, a profound student of philosophy, a writer of books, a man whose pure ideals and enthusiasms were an inspiration to everyone who knew him." As Barker wrote in her introduction to Letters From a Living Dead Man, *she transcribed the notes while in a state of semi-consciousness and hoped they would help others to no longer fear death, and to gain a sense of "exultant immortality."*

THE WAND OF WILL

NOT yet do you grasp the full mystery of will. It can make of you anything you choose, within the limit of your unit energy, for everything is either active or potential in the unit of force which is man.

The difference between a painter and a musician, or between a poet and a novelist, is not a difference of qualities in the entity itself; for each unit contains everything except quantity, and thus has the possibilities of development along any line chosen by its will. The choice may have been made ages ago. It takes a long time, often many lives, to evolve an art or a faculty for one particular kind of work in preference to all others. Concentration is the secret of power, here as elsewhere.

As to the use of will-power in your present everyday problems, there are two ways of using the will. One may concentrate upon a definite plan, and bring it into effect or not according to the amount of force at one's disposal; or one may will that the best and highest and wisest plan possible shall be demonstrated by the subconscious forces in the self and in other selves. The latter is a commanding of all environment for a special purpose, instead of commanding, or attempting to command, a fragment of it.

In this communion between the outer and inner worlds, you in the outer world are apt to think that we in ours know everything. You expect us to prophesy like fortune-tellers, and to keep you informed of what is passing on the other side of the globe. Sometimes we can; generally we cannot.

After a while I may be able to enter your mind as a Master does, and to know all the antecedent thoughts and plans in it; but now I cannot always do so.

For instance, one night I looked everywhere for—and could not find him. Perhaps it is necessary for you to think strongly of us, to make the way easiest.

I am learning all the time. The Teacher is very active in helping me.

When I am absolutely certain of my hold upon your hand, I shall have much to say about the life out here.

A LIGHT BEHIND THE VEIL

MAKE an opening for me sometimes in the veil of dense matter that shuts you from my eyes, I see you often as a spot of vivid light, and that is probably when your soul is active with feeling or your mind keen with thought.

I can read your thoughts occasionally, but not always. Often I try to draw near, and cannot find you. You could not always find me, perhaps, should you come out here.

Sometimes I am all alone: sometimes I am with others.

Strange, but I seem to myself to have quite a substantial body now, though at first my arms and legs seemed sprawling in all directions.

As a rule, I do not walk about as formerly, nor do I fly exactly, for I have never had wings; but I manage to get over space with incredible rapidity. Sometimes, though, I walk.

Now, I want you to do me a favour. You know what a difficult job I often had to keep things going, yet I kept them going. Don't you get discouraged about the material wherewithal for your work. Work right ahead, as if the supply were there, and it will be there. You can demonstrate it in one way or another. Do not feel weak or uncertain, for when you do you drag me back to earth by force of sympathy. It is as bad as grieving for the dead.

DON'T FORGET TO HYDRATE

YOU have been curious, perhaps, as to what we eat and drink, if anything. We certainly are nourished, and we seem to absorb much water. You also should drink plenty of water. It feeds the astral body. I do not think that a very dry body would ever have enough astral vitality to lend a hand to a soul on this plane of life, as you are doing now. There is much moisture in our bodies over here. Perhaps that is one reason why contact with a so-called spirit sometimes gives warm-blooded persons a sense of cold, and they shiver.

INDIVIDUAL HELLS

SOME time ago I told you of my intention to visit hell; but when I began investigations on that line there proved to be many hells. Each man who is not content with the orthodox hell of fire and brimstone builds one out of mind-stuff suited to his imaginative need. I believe that men place themselves in hell, that no God puts them there. I began looking for a hell of fire and brimstone, and found it. Dante must have seen the same things I saw. But there are other and individual hells—

(The writing suddenly stopped, for no apparent reason, and was not continued that night.)

THE GAME OF MAKE-BELIEVE

ONE day I met a man in doublet and hose, who announced to me that he was Shakespeare. Now I have become accustomed to such announcements, and they do not surprise me as they did six or eight months ago. (Yes, I still keep account of your months, for a purpose of my own.)

I asked this man what proof he could adduce of his extraordinary claim, and he answered that it needed no proof.

"That will not go down with me," I said, "for I am an old lawyer."

Thereupon he laughed, and asked: "Why did you not join in the game?"

I am telling you this rather senseless story, because it illustrates an interesting point in regard to our life here.

In a former letter I wrote about my meeting with a newly arrived lady, who, finding me dressed in a Roman toga, thought that I might be Caesar; and that I told her we were all actors here. I meant that, like children, we "dress up" when we want to impress our own imagination, or to relive some scene in the past.

This playing of a part is usually quite innocent, though sometimes the very ease with which it is done brings with it the temptation to deception, especially in dealings with the earth people.

You see the point I wish to make. The "lying spirits," of which the frequenters of seance rooms so often make complaint, are these astral actors, who may even come to take a certain pride in the cleverness of their art.

Be not too sure that the spirit who claims to be your deceased grandfather is that estimable old man himself. He may be merely an actor playing a part, for his own entertainment and yours.

How is one to tell, you ask? One cannot always tell. I should say, however, that the surest test of all would be the deep and unemotional conviction that the veritable entity was in one's presence. There is an instinct in the human heart which will never deceive us, if we without fear or bias will yield ourselves to its decision. How often in worldly matters have we all acted against this inner monitor, and been deceived and led astray!

If you have an instinctive feeling that a certain invisible—or even visible—entity is not what it claims to be, it is better to discontinue the conference. If it is the real person, and if he has anything vital to say, he will come again and again; for the so-called dead are often very desirous to communicate with the living.

As a rule, though, the play-acting over here is innocent of intent to deceive. Most men desire occasionally to be something which they are not. The poor man who, for one evening, dresses himself in his best clothes and squanders a week's salary in playing the millionaire is moved by the same impulse which inspired the man in my story to assert that he was Shakespeare. The woman who always dresses beyond her means is playing the same little game with herself and with the world.

All children know the game. They will tell you in a convinced tone that they are Napoleon Bonaparte, or George Washington, and they feel hurt if you scoff.

Perhaps my friend with the Shakespearean aspiration was an amateur dramatist when he was on earth. Had he been a professional dramatist, he would probably have stated his real name, more or less unknown, and followed it by the declaration that he was the well-known So-and-so.

There is much pride out here in the accomplishments of the

earth-life, especially among those who have recently come out. This lessens with time, and after one has been long here one's interests are likely to be more general.

Men and women do not cease to be human merely by crossing the frontier of what you call the invisible world. In fact, the human characteristics are often exaggerated, because the restraints are fewer. There are no penalties inflicted by the community for the personating of one man by another. It is not taken seriously, for to the clearer sight of this world the disguise is too transparent.

THE LEISURE OF THE SOUL

ONE of the joys of being here is the leisure for dreaming and for getting acquainted with oneself.

Of course there is plenty to do; but though I intend to go back to the world in a few years, I feel that there is time to get acquainted with myself. I tried to do that on earth, more or less; but here there are fewer demands on me. The mere labour of dressing and undressing is lighter, and I do not have to earn my living now, nor anybody else's.

You, too, could take time to loaf, if you thought you could. You can do practically anything you think you can do.

I purpose, for instance, in a few years not only to pick up a general knowledge of the conditions of this four-dimensional world, but to go back over my other lives and assimilate what I learned in them. I want to make a synthesis of the complete experiences of my ego up to this date, and to judge from that synthesis what I can do in the future with least resistance. I believe, but am not quite sure, that I can bring back much of this knowledge with me when I am born again.

I shall try to tell you—or some of you—when and about where to look for me again. Oh, don't be startled! It will not be for some time yet. An early date would necessitate hurry, and I do not wish to hurry. I could probably force the coming back, but that would be unwise, for I should then come back with less power than I want. Action and reaction being opposite and equal, and the unit, or ego, being able to generate only *so much* energy in a given time, it is better for me to rest in this condition of light matter until I have accumulated energy enough to come back with power. I shall not do, however, as many souls do; they stay out here until they are as tired of this world as they formerly were tired of the earth, and then are driven back half unconsciously by the irresistible force of the tide of rhythm. I want to guide that rhythm.

Since I have been here one man whom I know has gone back to the earth. He was about ready to go when I first found him. The strange part of it was that he himself did not understand his condition. He complained of being tired of things and of wanting to rest much. That was probably a natural instinct for rest, in preparation for the supreme effort of opening the doors of matter again. It is easy to come out here, but it requires some effort to go *from* this world into yours.

I know where that soul is now, for the Teacher told me. I had spoken to the Teacher about him, but he already knew of his existence. It was rather strange, for the man was one in whom I should have fancied that the Teacher would have taken little interest. But one never knows. Perhaps in his next life he may really begin to study the philosophy which *they* teach.

But I was speaking of the larger leisure out here. I wish you could arrange your life so as to have a little more leisure. I do not want you to be lazy, but the passive conditions of the mind are quite as valuable as the active conditions. It is when you are passive that we can reach you. When your mind and body are always occupied, it is difficult to impress you with any message of the soul. Find a little more time each day for doing nothing at all. It is good to do nothing sometimes; then the semi-conscious parts of your mind can work. They can remind you that there is an inner life; for the inner life that is "capable" to you on earth is really the point of contact with the world in which we live. I have said that the two worlds touch, and they touch through the inner. You go in to come out. It is a paradox, and paradoxes conceal great truths. Contradictions are not truths, but a paradox is not a contradiction.

There is a great difference in the length of time that people stay out here. You talk of being homesick. There are souls here who are homesick for the earth. They sometimes go back almost at once, which is generally a mistake. Unless one is young and still has a store of unused energy saved over from the last life, in going back to the earth too soon one lacks the force of a strong rebound.

It is strange to see a man here as homesick for the earth as certain poets and dreamers on earth are homesick for the inner life.

This use of the terms "outer" and "inner" may seem confusing; but you must remember that while you go in to come to us, we go out to come to you. In our normal state here we are living almost a subjective life. We become more and more objective as we touch your world. You become more and more subjective as you touch our world. If you only knew it, you could come to us at almost any time for a brief visit—I mean, by going deep enough into yourself.

If you want to try the experiment and will not be afraid, I can take you out here without your quite losing consciousness in your body—I mean without your being in deep sleep. You can call me when you want to make a trial. If I do not come at once, do not be discouraged. Of course at the moment I might be doing something else; but in that case I will come at another time.

There is no hurry. That is what I want to impress upon you. What you do not do this year you can perhaps do next year; but if you are always rushing after things, you can accomplish little in this particular work. Eternity is long enough for the full development of the ego of man. Eternity seems to have been designed for that end. That was a sound statement which was given at one time: "The object of life is life." I have realised that more fully since I had an opportunity to study eternity from a new angle. This is a very good angle from which to view both time and eternity. I see now what I did not see before, that I myself have never wasted any time. Even my failures were a valuable part of my experience. We lose to gain again. We go in and out of power sometimes as we go in and out of life, to learn what is there and outside. In this, as in all things, the object of life is life.

Do not hurry. A man may grow gradually into power and knowledge, or he may take them by force. Will is free. But the gradual growth has a less powerful reaction.

AN UNEXPECTED WARNING

I SHOULD be very sorry if the reading of these letters of mine should cause foolish and unthinking people to go spirit-hunting, inviting into their human sphere the irresponsible and often lying elemental spirits. Tell them not to do it.

My coming in this way through your hand is quite another matter. I could not do it if I had not been instructed in the scientific method of procedure, and I also could not do it if you should constantly interrupt me by side-thoughts of your own, and by questions relevant or irrelevant. It is because you are perfectly passive and not even curious, letting me use your hand as on earth I would have used the hand of my stenographer, that I am able to write long and connected sentences.

Most spirit communications, even when genuine, have little value, for the reason that they are nearly always coloured by the mind of the person through whom they pass.

You are right in reading nothing on the subject while these messages are coming, and in thinking nothing about this plane of life where I am. Thus you avoid preconceived ideas, which would interrupt the flow of my ideas.

You know, perhaps, that while on earth I investigated spiritualism, as I investigated many things of an occult nature, looking always for the truth that was behind them; but I was convinced then, and I am now more than ever convinced, that, except for the scientific demonstration that such things can be—which, of course, has value as a demonstration only,—most spirit-hunting is not only a waste of time, but an absolute detriment to those who engage in it.

This may sound strange coming from a so-called "spirit," one who is actually at this time in communication with the world. If that is so, I cannot help it. If I seem inconsistent, then I seem so; that is all. But I wish to go on record as discouraging irresponsible mediumship.

If a person sitting for mediumship could be sure that at the other end of the psychic line there was an entity who had something sincere and important to say, and who really could use him or her to say it through, it would be another matter; but this world out here is full of vagrants, even as the earth. As this world is peopled largely from your world, it is inevitable that we have the same kind of beings that you have. They have not changed much in passing through the doors of death.

Would you advise any delicate and sensitive woman to sit down in the centre of Hyde Park, and invite the passing crowds to come and speak through her, or touch her, or mingle their magnetism with hers? You shudder. You would shudder more had you seen some of the things which I have seen.

Then, too, there is another class of beings here, the kind which we used to hear the Theosophists call elementals*. Now, there has been a lot of nonsense written about elementals; but take this for a fact: there are units of energy, units of consciousness, which correspond pretty closely to what the Theosophists understand by elementals. These entities are not, as a rule, very highly developed; but as the stage of earth life is the stage to which they aspire, and as it is the next inevitable stage in their evolution, they are drawn to it powerfully.

So do not be too sure that the entity which raps on your table or your cupboard is the spirit of your deceased grandfather. It may be merely a blind and very desirous entity, an eager consciousness, trying to use you to hasten its own evolution, trying to get into you or through you, so as to enjoy the earth and the coarser vibrations of the earth.

It may not be able to harm you, but, on the other hand, it may do you a great deal of harm. You had better discourage such attempts to break through the veil which separates you from them; for the veil is thinner than you think, and though you cannot see through it, you can feel through it.

Having said this, my duty in the matter is discharged; and the next time I come I can tell you a story, maybe, instead of giving you a lecture.

I really feel like an astral Scheherazade**; but I fear you would tire of me before a thousand-and-one nights were past. A thousand-and-one nights! Before that time I shall have gone on. No, I do not mean "died" again into another world beyond; but when I get through telling you what I desire you to know about my life here, I want to investigate other stars, if it shall be permitted.

I am like a young man who has lately inherited a fortune and has at last unlimited means and opportunity for travel. Though he might stay around home a few months, getting matters in shape and becoming adjusted to his new freedom of movement, yet the time would come when he would want to try his wings. I hope that is not a mixed metaphor; if so, you can edit me. I shall not feel hurt.

---

* *Theosophy was a religion founded in the late nineteenth century by Russian immigrant occultist, Helena Blavatsky.*

** *Scheherazade, as the spirit references, is a major female character and the storyteller in the Middle Eastern collection of folk tales,* One Thousand and One Nights.

PSYCHOGRAPHY: MARVELOUS MANIFESTATIONS OF PSYCHIC POWER THROUGH FRED P. EVANS

"The grave is no longer voiceless," proclaimed J. J. Owen, in this late nineteenth-century book. His subject, Fred P. Evans, had two spirits that loved using his hand.

Evans was born on June 9, 1862, in Liverpool, England. After working various jobs as a young man, particularly as a mariner, he ended up in America. By 1884 he discovered mediumship at a séance in San Francisco. He then visited other mediums, all of whom predicted he'd be a powerful psychic. So Evans made their predictions come true and dedicated himself to joining their ranks. After three months of struggles he nearly gave up, but then he discovered his gift for slate-writing—and much more.

"I found that each month improved my mediumship, and that one phase developed another, so that with my continued sittings I not only developed independent slate-writing but also automatic writing, rapping, clairaudience, clairvoyance, physical manifestations, and materialization, and have demonstrated all the above gifts to thousands in California," Evans explained.

He produced handwritten messages and illustrations from beyond through the spirit powers of John Gray and Stanley St. Clair, respectively.

The communication included here comes from Gray, along with several others who scribbled messages on a slate in various languages. The experience is introduced by Owen and includes his commentary. As for Gray, before he became a spirit he was a young English seafarer who began communicating with spirits in 1835. These voices advised him to sail to New York., where he became a Coast Guardsman and chatted with spirits who rapped on rocks and foretold events, like shipwrecks and seizures.

"I in turn would warn my mates, until they began to regard me as the Evil One when they saw these prophecies fulfilled," Gray explained from the Other Side—a place he joined in 1837, after drowning during an attempt to save the crew of a wrecked ship off the coast. His ghost career took off through various mediums until he eventually found Evans.

This 1886 slate includes messages from spirits of numerous nationalities, including Socrates and Johann Karl Friedrich Zöllner, a German astrophysicist and psychical investigator who had died in 1882.

A SLATE OF MANY LANGUAGES

On the third Sunday, September 25th, [1886] we were promptly on hand, as before. The slate containing our private mark was taken by Mr. Evans and first thoroughly rubbed on both sides with a cloth slightly dampened with his saliva—(not a very neat way of cleansing a slate, but Mr. Evans says the writing comes much more readily when the slates are thus prepared). He then handed the slate to us, and we (Mrs. Owen and the writer) were both fully satisfied that there was no writing upon the slate. From that moment the slate never left our hands, nor was it for an instant out of our sight. A small bit of slate pencil was placed upon the table, and we placed the slate over it, with our four hands resting thereon. Mr. Evans, sitting upon the opposite side of the table, touched the outer edge of the slate frame for a few moments, and then removed his hands entirely. In about five minutes loud raps signalled that the writing was finished. We raised the slate and found the under side covered as seen in the engraving.

Two other slates, which had been prepared in like manner and placed upon the floor, with a bit of pencil between, were found at the close of the séance written full. As the message purports to come from the controlling spirit, and relates to the main work in hand, we give it:

MY DEAR FRIENDS, MR. AND MRS. OWEN:—I see your object is to create an interest among skeptics of spiritual phenomena and cause them to investigate. I entered in with your feelings, and have succeeded in inducing twelve spirits of different nationality to write a few words in the language they used when on earth. You will, no doubt, find many defects, but we have done the best we can, and you must accept it with the knowledge that these spirits never wrote through the medium before; therefore, they are at a disadvantage; and there is also a difficulty in bringing them here to write, for, as you will understand, there is no attraction for them. But I have the medium, yourself and wife, for an attraction. You will see that the languages written embrace Chinese, Japanese, Egyptian, Old Asiatic, Hebrew, German, Italian, French, Spanish, Greek, Norwegian and English. Wishing your dear wife, yourself and the *Golden Gate* every prosperity, I am your friend and well wisher in spirit,

— JOHN GRAY

Of the messages given there are some defects, as Mr. Gray says may be expected; but on the whole we regard the writing as most remarkable, the Asiatic languages especially, of which but very few of our own race have ever acquired anything more than an imperfect speaking knowledge. A learned professor, who assisted in the translations, thinks there is not a scholar in San Francisco who can write all the languages given upon this slate. Following are the translations of the writings:

German—I have found an easy way for making known to science the proof of the return of the dead to this earth, and I shall soon give it to the world. —Professor Zöllner.

Italian— I am glad to be able to write you a few lines to aid in proving the truth of a future life. —Count Rozzia.

French—Monsieur Gray.—I have acquitted myself of your commission. —M. Fremont.

Greek—I come to say this—seek for better things—think well of all. —Socrates.

Spanish—My Dear Friend, Sr. Don Orven:—Rich or wise as a man may be, don't let him be proud. It is from a King, Agesilaus, we have that grand maxim, "that one is not great only as far as he is just." —Don Juan Alviso.

Norwegian—I am here. —Herr Holle.

Chinese—I write a few words for you. —Lu Yeun.

Japanese—How do you do? —Oyama Centura.

Hebrew—[This is a name of a book, describing the killing of animals according to the Jewish rites.]

The writing in the upper left hand corner is claimed to be Egyptian, which we were unable to translate. We submitted the matter to John Gray, when he wrote the following: "I give it to you as received by me. The Egyptian reads: 'Yea, the spirit of man shall live forever. —Nefo;' who was an old Egyptian seer."

The cuneiform characters just below the Egyptian comprise the letters of the words "Tom Paine."

> My Dear Friend Mr. Owen:—I have succeeded in bringing the above spirit friends together and inducing them to write a few words in their earthly language, as a test of spirit return. This is the best we can do. Good-bye.
> — JOHN GRAY

To set at rest any idea that may be entertained that this writing was a transference from our own minds, we will say that with the exception of some little knowledge of French and less of Spanish, the English language is the only language with which we are familiar. We positively know that the writing was not clone by any mortal hand. As we have in our possession the slate upon which it was written, any one interested can satisfy himself that the writing is by no chemical preparation, as the fine particles of slate caused by the attrition of the pencil over the surface of the slate can readily be seen.

We have given, in the above statement, the simple facts; the skeptical reader may explain them as best he may.

THE
Encyclopædia of Death

AND

LIFE IN THE SPIRIT-WORLD.

OPINIONS AND EXPERIENCES FROM EMINENT SOURCES.

By J. R. FRANCIS.

Author of "Search After God," "Is the Devil Dead?" etc.

VOLUME I.

(FOURTH EDITION.)

CHICAGO:
THE PROGRESSIVE THINKER PUBLISHING HOUSE,
1903.

THE ENCYCLOPAEDIA OF DEATH AND LIFE IN THE SPIRIT-WORLD

The Progressive Thinker *was a Spiritualist newspaper and publisher of numerous books, including this encyclopedia of death. As it states in its introduction,* "The main object to be attained in The Encyclopaedia of Death, and Life in the Spirit-World, *is to so educate the masses that the last great event in the earthly career of each one will no longer be regarded with superstitious feelings, but on the contrary be looked upon as a beneficent ordinance of Nature, without which the world would soon be plunged into darkness and woe."*

If one believed all the messages of afterlife activity within its pages, the book would have succeeded. Its many voices from beyond assure its readers that death is nothing to fear. The selection included here offers a series of questions and answers with a loquacious spirit called Lucretus.

DEATH CONSIDERED BY SPIRIT LUCRETUS

Important Questions Comprehensively Answered.

LUCRETUS—I have come to you to respond to your questions.

INQUIRER—No subject is more worthy of the careful and serious attention of mortals than that of death, and I desire such information thereon from you as you may see fit to impart. You, of course, passed through the change called death?

LUCRETUS—Most assuredly, sir. No one can escape from passing through that glorious change which causes the soul to emerge from the material side of life and enter the spiritual realms. My transit to Spirit-life was caused by consumption, and I gave the various stages through which I passed a careful and critical examination. Under the influence of that disease, my mind retained its ordinary brilliancy to the last—indeed, it became, at times, grandly illuminated, and I caught a glimpse of the Spirit-world, though I regarded the scenes presented to my vision as fantasms of the brain—illusions resulting from extreme nervous prostration. I died gradually, like the fading of a glorious summer day, or the expiring of a lighted taper.

INQUIRER—Indeed, sir, your experiences are worthy of being recorded in the pages of history.

LUCRETUS—During my sickness I learned an important lesson. When first prostrated by disease, I weighed 175 pounds, and after suffering therefrom several months, I only weighed 93; and before my spirit was freed from its prison cage, 1 was reduced to 75 pounds in weight; 100 pounds of my body had already died—passed away, vanished, no one knew whither! This gradual waste consisted in the dispersion of many of the molecules that composed my system, through regular disintegration or sloughing off. In health, all the molecules of the body are harmoniously wedded; but in sickness, they are placed in discordant relations. One hundred pounds of my system, at a certain period of my sickness, no longer existed in connection with my organism. Mortals would say, then, that only 75 pounds of the original 175 died, for I weighed the former when I finally passed away. The molecules of my body continued to be dissipated so long as my spirit remained attached to it, when finally the vital forces were completely exhausted.

INQUIRER—Please explain what you mean by a molecule.

LUCRETUS—Sir William Thomson, the distinguished scientist, introduces a very pretty example of the size and nature of a molecule. He imagines a single drop of water to be magnified until it becomes as large as the earth, having a diameter of 8,000 miles, and all the molecules to be magnified in the same proportion; and then concludes that a single molecule will appeal, under these circumstances, as somewhat larger than a shot, and somewhat smaller than a cricket ball. Each molecule may be composed of two or more atoms, and it is the smallest portion of matter that can exist in a free or uncombined state. Now imagine, if you please, that the body is composed of particles of matter the size of a marble; continue to dwell upon it with the mind's eye, diminishing it in size, until it disappears from the natural eye, but through the instrumentality of the microscope you are still able to prove its existence. Continue to decrease its dimensions until your microscope will no longer render it visible. Though reduced in size and not visible to the eye aided by the microscope,—it still exists as a molecule, of which the human organism is composed; like a house constructed of bricks; each brick as a molecule could be seen by the eye; but those which compose the body, when separated, become invisible. In the aggregate, you can see them, as you can a drop of water. You deal altogether with matter; we with both matter and spirit, and when I tell you that the human system is composed of innumerable molecules, and that each molecule contains several atoms held together by attractive forces, and that all of them, under certain circumstances, are subservient to the indwelling spirit, then, even, you can hardly realize the fact. Within the system animals are constantly being evolved. Some of them are plainly visible to the naked eye. Others can be brought to light through the aid of a microscope, while there are millions so very small that the mortal eye will never be favored with a sight of them. There is not an animal in existence that a form resembling it cannot be found in the physical organism. Could you see them in the putrid fevers, gaze at their manoeuvers in loathsome ulcers, or behold their various motions when the system is in perfect health, you would be astonished. Please bear these thoughts in mind, for I shall frequently allude to them hereafter.

INQUIRER—What were your sensations during your sickness?

LUCRETUS—Peculiar, indeed. My mind grew brilliant just in the proportion that the molecules left my body. When 100 pounds of them had vanished, gone on other missions, my mind was, at times, beautifully illuminated, and I not only saw spirits surrounding me, but I beheld the magnificent scenery of the Spirit-world.

INQUIRER—Did you realize that you saw spirits and the scenery of the Spirit-world?

LUCRETUS—No, not at the time. I thought that it was all an illusion. During my sickness, I lived in dream-land, as it were. Birds of beautiful plumage and gaudy colors; celestial beings dressed in elegant attire; and picturesque scenes of different kinds, were constantly before me. In proportion as I grew weak, my mind became illuminated. When the body is dead, as you term it, the spirit can by no possibility remain attached to it. The last I remember in connection with my disease, I heard my attendant physician declare that I was dead. I seemed then to sink down, as if falling from a high mountain, and in a moment I became unconscious. When I awoke, I was surrounded by my friends in the Spirit-world. Since that memorable period, I have witnessed many deaths.

INQUIRER—Was not your death accompanied with great pain?

LUCRETUS—None whatever. Generally a person is unconscious when passing through certain stages of death, though not always. While on earth, the spirit is compelled to assume a dress corresponding with the plane on which it lives. You are simply a materialized spirit—so substantial is its outer form, that it only vanishes through gradual disintegration or decomposition. When a spirit returns to earth and enters the sphere or aura of a physical medium, it becomes a central attractive point. Allow me to say that there proceeds from each person an emanation, partaking of every characteristic of each organ of the body. That emanation I regard as the sphere, radiating influence, or aura. In physical mediums it is very dense. I enter the aura of a physical medium, and each organ of my spirit body attracts therefrom a material which corresponds with each physical organ. Around my spiritual eye, a retina, cornea, and optic nerve are formed, connecting with the brain. In connection with my spiritual ear, a material auditory nerve is constructed, which enables me to hear different earthly sounds. This process continues until I have a genuine physical system corresponding with the plane on which you live. Now, when that organism disintegrates, it returns to the medium from whom I procured it. When your physical system disintegrates, or decomposes, it returns to the earth, whence obtained. I have often assumed a material form since I passed from earth. In so doing, I can come in contact with matter, and to a certain extent control it, which I could not do otherwise. When I surrender my materialized form to the medium from whom it is temporarily borrowed, I am then immediately transferred to the spirit side of life, but in no case is it death. When conditions are favorable, it is as easy to form a physical covering for the spirit, as it is to make water from invisible gases. Water, you well know, can be decomposed, rendered invisible to the eye, yet in a flash it can be brought back to its original state, and adapted to the use of man.

INQUIRER—You, then, take the position there is really no death?

LUCRETUS—Death is only change. The world to-day, in some respects at least, reasons to very little purpose. The opinion generally entertained that death is something terrible, and always to be avoided, is without a particle of foundation. It is a most desirable change, transferring each one to the spirit side of life. During my protracted sickness, my dreams and visions were beautiful. The grandeur of the Spirit-world frequently delighted my enraptured vision, and my soul seemed to float in the aroma of spirit flowers. Angelic music thrilled my soul, and gave me a foretaste of Spirit-life. Angelic children came and spread flowers on my bed, sang their sweet songs, and enveloped me with their hallowed influence. In fact, it was delightful to die. The presence of these children, so pure, lovely and innocent, shed over me a silvery light that only spirit eyes could see.

INQUIRER—Can a spirit pass through the death-scene as often as desirable?

LUCRETUS—I have heard it frequently discussed in the Spirit-world. I do not believe it impossible; indeed, I have long since ceased to cry humbug! at even the most exaggerated declarations and statements in reference to what can be accomplished by the power and skill of man or spirits. Glance for a moment at the physical mechanism of a sheep. It roams over the rich pasturage, nips the tender blade of grass, laves its thirst in the running brook, and breathes the fresh air, and strange to say a coat of snowy whiteness comes forth on its body. The complex, chemical laboratory of the animal manufactured the wool from grass, water and the atmosphere. When a little lamb it only weighed five pounds, but now it weighs seventy. From those three sources, its chemical laboratory extracted sixty-five pounds of mutton. This is, indeed, astonishing, how an animal weighing only five pounds can finally become such a self-acting manufacturing establishment, making from ten to fifteen pounds of wool a year. Now, in elucidation of my subject, I desire to say that it is possible to go direct to the elements and make wool therefrom. You on earth who desire wool to form various fabrics, must procure sheep to produce it for you. They go to the grass, etc., for it; and were you wise enough you could go there, too. Look at the butterfly with its gaudy colors; at the birds of the air with their beautiful plumage. Each one carries a different chemical laboratory. *That which* can create, evolve, or form a bird, must as a natural consequence understand all about the chemical apparatus it carries, and must be superior thereto. *That which* can construct the butterfly, with its variegated hues, must necessarily thoroughly comprehend the blending of colors. *That which* can bring into existence a seed that can germinate and unfold a beautiful blossom, must be an excellent florist. In fact, *That which* creates animals that can produce wool, milk, soft fur, beautiful feathers, etc., from grass, must be able to accomplish the same thing, himself, herself, or *itself* without any aid from them whatever. Now, I am not required to go to *That which*, the great Creative Power, to find the skill requisite to evolve articles of diet. Chemists in Spirit-life already understand that process. When this earth shall have become so densely populated that animals must be dispensed with, that knowledge will be imparted to earth's children, which will enable them to go direct to *the source* for a supply of milk, butter, fruits, etc. That intellect must, indeed, be narrow in comprehension that does not consider the human mind superior to the *body* of the sheep, bird or cow. I know that it is possible for a spirit to assume a physical body, which it obtains from certain elements. The time will come, I think, when it can be so materialized as to be retained indefinitely. Materialization is yet in its infancy. Ten years will work marvelous changes. If a spirit assume a physical organization, it must be dissipated before it can again enter Spirit-life. Of course, such would be death to the body organized.

INQUIRER—Your ideas are peculiar, sir, in relation to this question.

LUCRETUS—Puny child of earth, how narrow your comprehension! Of the sublime realities of the sciences, as existing in Spirit-life, you and the denizens of earth know comparatively nothing. If Mr. Field of the Atlantic cable notoriety could stand in New York, and with a battery no larger than a thimble, and with only one drop of water, move a piece of iron in England (the hammer for telegraphing), what estimate do you put upon the power of him who has been in Spirit-life for 100,000 years?* Indeed, it is towering, grand!

INQUIRER—Will the time ever arrive when death will not occur?

LUCRETUS—The earth will ultimately become so spiritualized and refined, that when *death* takes place, the consciousness will probably be retained throughout. The earth is exceedingly gross yet, and the emanations therefrom are not favorable for advanced spiritual growth and development. The conditions now, however, are just what are absolutely required. The ancient saurian monsters could not live in the atmosphere of to-day a single moment. Their gross natures required gross conditions. Those human beings who first inhabited the earth plane, living in caves and holes in the ground, could not survive a month if alive at this time. The physical condition of this planet is gradually improving, and as it advances, the human race steps forward and assumes a higher condition. The physical form of to-day is far less gross than that which existed twenty thousand years ago. Physical man has nothing whatever to do with the motion of the earth in space; nothing whatever to do with its advancement in the refining process which is constantly going on. But he moves grandly along, advancing just as rapidly as its physical condition will permit. The time will arrive when the physical body will become so spiritualized that there will be but little resemblance between it and those possessed by mortals at present. Death then will lose all of its terrors.

INQUIRER—Cannot partial death of the body occur?

LUCRETUS—A portion of the brain may be removed, and still the vigor of the mind be not impaired in the least. The arms and legs may be amputated, the eyes destroyed, the auditory nerves rendered useless, the tongue severed from the mouth, and other parts of the body cut off, yet life remains, and the brain loses none of its brilliancy. Your external covering—the outer dress of the spirit—is composed of innumerable molecules, which are extracted from the food you eat, water you drink, and air you breathe, and therein may be found all the constituents of the animal, vegetable and mineral kingdoms. There are animalculae in your body resembling in a marked degree the lizard, snake, worm, etc., etc., and therein the great mystery of man's organic structure lies. Let the mother, who is nursing in the womb an embryonic child, be frightened by a snake at a certain period of gestation, and she arouses thereby all the molecules in her body which are in the form of that animal, and in consequence of their increased action, they so change the shape of the being she is developing, that when it is born, it resembles a snake! To demonstrate the potent character of molecular influence, I would refer you to an incident that occurred in San Francisco, Cal., where a lady, Mrs. Jervis, was bitten by a poisonous tarantula. She lingered for six months in continual agony, her blood literally drying up, till she was reduced to an absolute skeleton. Three months before her death her entire right side became paralyzed; yet, strange to say, the hand had a tendency to crawl, and the fingers incessantly moved like the legs of a spider. I tell you, further, that the animalculae of the system, in the form of animals, generate the virus that causes hydrophobia when induced by fear, the impulse of the mind, or by the bite of a rabid dog. These molecules are obedient, under certain circumstances, to the action of the mind. You have heard of men who have hoggish dispositions; in them animalculae in the form of hogs predominate; in others that of ferocious beasts, and they are pugilists; in the murderer animals of prey are the ruling power; in the man or woman who is snappish, mean, and quarrelsome in disposition—those animalculae are in the ascendency that represent such traits of character. This is one of the grandest truths in existence.

No longer fear death! It opens the portals of the celestial world, and presents to you a home, beautiful and grand. Remember, too, that you can refine your spiritual nature only by generous acts and high resolves. As the thought of hydrophobia will often induce that disease in its aggravated form, so will the contemplation of committing murder prepare one for the desperate deed. The thinking of doing wrong arouses the rapacious, passionate molecules of the body and places one in a condition where he is forced to do some bad deed. A man nurses the intention of committing rape until his body moves him irresistibly along to do it. He whose mind is pure never arouses to activity the insatiate animals of his nature, and he develops the angel within himself. I appeal to all, then, who wish to take an advanced position in the Spirit-world, to have their whole life distinguished by good deeds and philanthropic purposes. Life is short on earth at most, and the improvements there made are felt throughout all eternity.

---

* Lucretus refers to Cyrus West Field, an American businessman and financier who helped create the Atlantic Telegraph Company and lay the first telegraph cable across the Atlantic Ocean in 1858.

AUTOMATIC

— OR —

SPIRIT WRITING,

WITH OTHER

PSYCHIC EXPERIENCES,

— BY —

SARA A. UNDERWOOD.

WITH AN INTRODUCTION BY B. F. UNDERWOOD.

CHICAGO, ILL.
PUBLISHED BY THOMAS G. NEWMAN,
147 South Western Avenue.
1896.

AUTOMATIC OR SPIRIT WRITING, WITH OTHER PSYCHIC EXPERIENCES

The following conversations showcase just a few of the communications Sara A. Underwood had with spirits toward the end of the nineteenth century. She and her husband, Benjamin Franklin Underwood, asked the questions and her hand recorded the answers.

"She has, to my positive knowledge, written in this automatic way, statements which included matter-of-fact information, unknown to her and unknown to me, showing that the intelligence which supplied the thought and controlled the hand to write, had access to sources of knowledge beyond the conscious reach of the psychic," Mr. Underwood wrote in their book's introduction. "These are curious facts."

Sara Underwood, an early feminist, was also known to write without the help of the dead. She was an avid writer of essays, stories, and poems. But despite her skills as a wordsmith, her husband maintained every word captured through automatic writing was authentic.

"The messages received automatically, in every case that has come under my observation," he claimed. They came, he added, from spirits "that once dwelt in the flesh, now discarnate and freed from material conditions."

A Q&A ON THE NATURE OF DEATH

Q.—From your standpoint, do you consider death the end of conscious existence?
A.—Death, we know only as a phrase used to indicate change of environment.

Q.—Is death expected on your plane, as on ours, or do you all understand that the next change is progress?
A.—Slow even are those on our plane to understand the law of unending evolution.

Q.—When one enters into your sphere—when we are called dead—is there at first a period of unconsciousness; or is there an unbroken consciousness, a remembrance of what has transpired?
A.—When what you call death occurs—which is really a new birth—unconsciousness is the stage of transition; but, as soon as the newborn spirit is found strong enough to understand the very natural change which has taken place—a change which, if he or she has been an observer of the thousands of metamorphoses occuring in earth life with lower forms, will seem the most natural possible in evolution—then the knowledge of such change dawns upon the sense-perceptions, and all becomes clear.

SPIRIT WORLD FAQs

Q.—How long in our time is it before a spirit passed from our plane to yours comes to consciousness?
A.—When born into Spirit-life the period of what is akin to mind growth on your plane varies according to previous conditions of heredity as with children—so we cannot predict.

Q.—Do you in your sphere require any sort of food or nourishment to supply waste of force, as we require for the upbuilding of our bodies?
A.—Spirit comes not by outward accretion, but proceeds to develop from within.

Q.—Can you make that answer more clear to our perception?
A.—Show you that each process of evolution whether spiritual or physical depends upon the germinating power within it.
Q.—Can you indicate from whence comes that germinating power.
A.—Sense knowledge is so undeveloped so far as spiritual workings are given in your sphere, that no definite answer can be given, but when you understand all the forces which are at work from the formation of an acorn to an oak, we will then clearly explain the evolutionary processes of spirit arising from your sense plane.

Q.—Do you in your spheres have one language, or what corresponds therewith, or many as we here have?
A.—Spiritual language does not correspond with your vague ideas, but we will try to give you symbolically an idea of language as we know it. Spirit language means only Thought, a word coined by man to express something inexpressible to those on your static knowledge; so all languages are but symbolic parts of spirit speech, and virtually we have but one language, which includes all which you have differentiated. Your languages are dialects only.

Q.—Do you have habitations distinct and separate from others—like our homes here?
A.—What are your homes—give us some idea of what you mean.
Q.—Home to us means the private refuge of congenial minds.
A.—Thou sayest well—then do we spirits more than you have real homes.
Q.—Explain more fully what you mean.
A.—Spiritual soul relationship goes deeper and is pointedly superior to mere blood relationship as ye shall understand when your sense conditions are of no further use.

Q.—Do you have any need of what we call apparel—clothes?
A.—Choose ye what apparel shall be yours. Thou shouldst understand that in the spirit-world clothing typifies the state of those who choose their raiment. Our friend who gave the world our thought in Sartor Resartus spoke better than he knew in saying clothes signify humanity.

Q.—Can you tell us what your methods of locomotion are?

A.—Travel with us depends on the need or desire.
Q.—Then you do go from place to place?
A.—Oh, yes, and with more rapidity than is possible on your planet.

Q.—What can you tell us as to the locality of your sphere?
A.—There are no words in your language which we can make useful. Verbal words of expression are inadequate to express that of which there is no equivalent on your plane.

Q.—Do you have your hours of sleep there?
A.—Sleep, as you understand it, is unknown to us.

Q.—Have you greater opportunities there for study and learning than when here?
A.—Knowledge here is on an altogether different basis than with you, but we have delightful opportunities and wealth of spiritual roadway.

Q.—Do you on your plane have anything analogous to our idea of individual ownership of property, or is not your plane rather on the line of ownership of properties—qualities?
A.—Thou art right. There is on soul planes no cognition of selfish ownership of anything spiritual; spirits are of right owners of all good, but temporal earthly goods are here accounted buzzards' prey.

Q.—What is the personal possession of one individual spirit in distinction from the possessions of other spirits?
A.—Spiritual possessions are always marked by boundless desire to make those possessions the common property of all.
Q.—What then is the greatest good or possession of spirit life?
A.—Shall we now repeat what so often thou hast been told?
Q.—If necessary, yes.
A.—Self must be submerged. Jesus said: "Do unto others as thou would'st be done by."
Q.—On your plane does any one own what we call personal property?
A.—None of tradesman sort.
Q.—What marks individual belongings on your side?
A.—Craving personal belongings is characteristic of your earthly experience.
Q.—Do all on leaving this plane lose all desire for individual property?

A.—Thou should'st ask—Are all who leave your phase of existence endowed with sufficient knowledge of spiritual brotherhood to commence with those spirits who are far in advance of untried souls, to overcome selfish—that is earthly—greed?

Q.—Do you have a desire to communicate with those still in the body?
A.—Salvation of troubled souls gives us power to benefit, and that is our wealth.

Q.—Are the unsatisfied longings of this life satisfied on your plane?
A.—Yes. Wants are here generally satisfied.

Q.—On your plane do you still continue to take interest in the sciences which you studied while in earth form, or does your change of state change the trend of your investigations?
A.—Science with us, as with you, widens our knowledge of natural laws. When you join our scientific society here you will change your estimate of some people.

Q.—Do you mean that your science deals more with character than with things?
A.—Your estimate of scientific knowledge is based upon your earthly sense relations; you know what Jesus said, "A little child shall lead them."

Q.—Do you have there your seasons of rest, equivalent to our sleep?
A.—Our ideas of rest are not like unto yours. When we rest we creep down to your level.

Q.—Can you explain sleep as we know it?
A.—Sleep is the silence of thought, the garnering of life's harvest. Sleep is not death's twin, but willingness converted into modes of rest.

Q.—What are dreams?
A.—Dreams are the percipients of life's experiences—shams of being.

Q.—What is character?
A.—Energies of mind. Mean only that one determines to be the best his ideal will allow.

Q.—Are the different religious beliefs held by men on our plane carried on to your sphere and believed in, after their death?
A.—Clear thinking is not at once attained by even the fairest minded

who experience the change you call death; and with new meanings attached to old ideas the sects still persist for one or more changes of planes.

Q.—Are all planets phases of the life of this earth?
A.—Planets are worlds such as this in many cases, but most frequently on a far different mode of existence with different sense relations.
Q.—Do beings on different planets have language akin to ours?
A.—No, for language, environments, evolutionary developments and sympathies are in all worlds different.
Q.—Do you in your sphere ever see or hold communication with beings belonging to other planets than this earth?
A.—Your ideas as to planets are so tinged and gauged by your circumscribed sense perceptions that you would regard what we know of other conditions as mere nonsense.
Q.—But can you not at least tell us whether the inhabitants of any planet are like us in form or intellectual conditions?
A.—Shadowy beings you would consider the sweet personalities who come from those planets with which our plane has mortal communication; but we know they are real beings, albeit on a far different basis, from yours and ours. Changed conditions make it impossible to state, or to clearly know, whether they are below or above us in intelligence.
Q.—Do spirits from different planets visit earth?
A.—Some do. Change the subject. There are certain limits to which spirits on your plane are bounded because it is thought best that men creep before walking.

Q.—Does cremation of the body after death interfere with spiritual conditions? Is earth burial preferable from your point of view?
A.—Cremation of the body doubtlessly is the most esthetic mode of disposing of the material habitation of spirit, and there is no partaking of body with spirit after dissolution. None at all, no more than when we leave one dwelling for another.
Q.—Then would you advise cremation in preference to burial?
A.—The mode of dissolution matters little. The freed spirit cares not whether its old shell decays by degrees, or instantaneously.
Q.—Does the form of man change with change of planes?

A.—Cannot you understand that your ideas of form are limited by your sense perceptions, and you could not understand the correct answer to your question!

Q.—Do class distinctions exist on your plane?
A.—Classes here are high or low according to the strength of moral worth, and also superior lovingness of all. Your companionship with mortals is based on their congeniality in some way with your moral and intellectual nature. So also with your companionship with souls on our plane.

Q.—Are the standards of merit on your plane identical with or similar to ours here?
A.—Souls are classed here according to their withstanding of the strongest temptations to which they are subjected on your plane. There are those here guilty of great crimes according to earthly codes who yet take precedence of some who had no temptation to sin.

Q.—Do family names and affinities persist?
A.—Years gone, by this question was seriously discussed among us and this conclusion was reached: that names with you were but the signs of tribal relations between those of mere blood-relationship; here, blood-relationship does not count, and spirit sympathies come always to be classified by new readings.

Q.—Are members of the same family drawn toward their own relations when they come to your sphere?
A.—Conditionally they are, but many times family relations are not as: pleasant as some other mode of personal magnetism would be.

Q.—Why is it that we get so few messages from our relatives in the Spirit-world in spite of our strong desire to do so?
A.—Bonds of sympathetic being are stronger than relationship over here. Many whose silence you wonder at were not in accord with you. True lines of sympathy are drawn over here. Blood relations are often hurtful, but soul relations will ever assert themselves and give joy when recognized. Bonds of spirit are stronger than man's paltry blood-relationship.

Q.—Do husband and wife continue lovers on your planes?
A.—If a man and woman—married, according to your ideas—are in

true rapport with each other, the change called death does not alter their relations, but if through misapprehension they are mismated, however desirous they may be of higher development, their ardent hopes count for naught if natural sympathy says no. Sympathies and antipathies are stronger here than with you, for here we separate the wheat from the chaff; we only care for the spirits who are at one with us. Changed conditions make new relations.

Q.—Do we still endure after the change called death?
A.—Sensitive souls endure what you call life. Spirits on our plane go on striving after blessed existence.

Q.—Does personality—one's individual selfhood persist on your plane?
A.—Personality does persist, but not as strongly as on earth. Each soul assimilates with its highest ideal and grows toward it, even as on earth you aspire to the best you can assimilate.

Q.—Will we, or anyone, individually obtain eternal life?
A.—Another upward step may shed light on the question just asked. As the poet says: "He knows. He knows!" We do not yet.

Q.—Is not every spirit on your plane assured of continued existence?
A.—Continued existence does not necessarily mean immortality to all mankind. When the change you call death occurs, there is but a step taken toward the change which annihilates as well as strengthens.

Q.—Does our personality continue through all planes of being or is it sometimes merged into one great all?
A.—Man's being is not as you fancy, some atom by itself but "all are but parts of one stupendous whole."
Q.—But on your plane does the individual persist with its personal loves, hates and idiosyncracies?
A.—Spirit life is life of the individual brought into harmony with those of the same sympathies.
Q.—With those whose moral nature attracts? whom they love?
A.—Yes, love is the great principle of man's being—Love.
Q.—Will you tell us if we have any pre-existence as conscious individuals, or does our individualism begin with our birth into this outer world?

A.—Placed as germs from a great fountain of soul life, your atomistic mortality as ego begins.

Q.—On your plane do you arrive at certainty in regard to immortality?
A.—We here are as ignorant as you are as to the ultimate of existence. Immortality is still an undetermined issue. One life at a time seems as pertinent with us as with you.

Psychic photography of William. T. Stead, 1915.

AFTER DEATH, OR LETTERS FROM JULIA

AND

THE BLUE ISLAND: EXPERIENCES OF A NEW ARRIVAL BEYOND THE VEIL

William T. Stead was a Victorian-era newspaper editor and journalist who got swept up in the London Spiritualism scene in the 1890s. But he didn't just attend séances and report about his experiences. Stead discovered he had his own psychic ability to receive direct messages from the dead through automatic writing.

His main contact was Julia A. Ames, an American journalist he'd befriended years earlier, but who had died on December 12, 1891. Long before her passing, she and a lifelong friend, Ellen, agreed that whoever went to the grave first would send messages to the other from beyond. Sure enough, Ellen claimed to have seen apparitions of Julia standing near her bedside. "I know it was Julia, and she has come back to me as she promised," Ellen told Stead. "But I could not hear her speak, and I cannot bear to think that she may have come back with a message for me, and yet I could not hear what she had to say."

Fortunately for Ellen and Julia, Stead was ready to help with his newfound psychography skills. "I offer, in case she were willing and able to use my hand as her own, to allow Julia to write what message she pleased by that means," Stead explained in the introduction to his book, After Death, or Letters From Julia.

Julia took him up on the offer and had plenty to say. "Sitting alone with a tranquil mind, I consciously placed my right hand, with the pen held in the ordinary way, at the disposal of Julia, and watched with keen and skeptical interest to see what it would write," Stead added.

The first batch of messages Stead received were for Ellen, but later messages were meant for publication to broader audiences.

According to Stead's daughter, Estella, the journalist and automatic writer's adventures in Spiritualism continued when he took his own trip beyond the veil. Stead's journey began when a voyage to the United States went unfinished. He was one of the more than 1,500 people who died on the Titanic in 1912. Surviving witnesses said Stead had helped women and children escape and gave away his life jacket.

Several years later, Pardoe Woodman, an acquaintance of Estella's, developed a knack for automatic writing and began channeling her father.

"Mr. Woodman never knew my father personally nor has he come into touch with his writing or with his work in any way, and yet the wording and the phrasing of the messages are my father's, and even the manner of writing is typical of him," Estella wrote in the preface to The Blue Island: Experiences of a New Arrival Beyond the Veil.

Included here are selections from Letters from Julia *and the first four chapters of Stead's own posthumous words.*

RETURN TO FRIENDS

I began to be sad about you, and I wanted to go back; the angel took me swiftly through the air to where I came from. When I entered the death-chamber there lay my body. It was no longer of interest to me, but I was so grieved to see how you were all weeping over my worn-out clothes, I wished to speak to you. I saw you, darling, all wet with tears, and I was so sad I could not cheer you.

THE LIFE BEYOND

I find it so difficult to explain how we live, and how we spend our time. We never weary, and do not need to sleep as we did on earth; neither do we need to eat or drink; these things were necessary for the material body; here we do not need them. I think we can best teach you what we experience by asking you to remember those moments of exaltation when, in the light of the setting or rising sun, you look out, happy and contented, upon the landscape over which the sun's rays have shed their magical beauty. There is peace; there is life; there is beauty; above all, there is love. Beauty everywhere, joy and love. Love, love is the secret of Heaven. God is love, and when you are lost in love you are found in God.

THE NOTHINGNESS OF THINGS

There is a thing that surprised me not a little, and that was, or is, the discovery of the nothingness of things. I mean that the entire nothingness of most things which seemed to one on earth the most important things. For instance, money, rank, worth, merit, station, and all the things we most prize when on earth, are simply nothing. They don't exist any more than the mist of yesterday or the weather of last year. They were no doubt influential for a time, but they do not last; they pass as the cloud passes, and are not visible any more.

WANTED, A BUREAU OF COMMUNICATION

What is wanted is a bureau of communication between the two sides. Could you not establish some such sort of office with one or more trustworthy mediums? If only it were to enable the sorrowing on earth to know, if only for once, that their so-called dead live nearer them than ever before, it would help to dry many a tear and soothe many a sorrow. I think you could count upon the co-operation of all on this side.

We on this side are full of joy at the hope of this coming to pass. Imagine how grieved we must be to see so many whom we love, sorrowing without hope, when those for whom they sorrow are trying in vain every means to make them conscious of their presence. And many also are racked with agony, imagining that their loved ones are lost in hell, when in reality they have been found in the all-embracing arms of the love of God. Ellen, dear, do talk of this with Minerva, and see what can be done. It is the most important thing there is to do. For it brings with it the trump of the Archangel, when those that were in their graves shall awake and walk forth once more among men.

THE DANGERS OF COMMUNICATING ACROSS THE BORDER

I want to say one word now about the danger of the communications about which you hear so much. I have not much to say. That there is love on this side is true. The devil and his angels are no mere metaphysical abstractions. There are evil ones, false ones, frivolous ones on this side, as there are on yours. You can never enlarge the scope and range of existence without at the same time enlarging the area of possible temptation and probable loss and peril. But the whole question is one of balance. And what I want to ask you is this, Do you or anyone else in your world ever cut off your communications with your children when they have gone into the larger life of a city, because they may bring you into the vortex of a city's temptations and the risk of evil and danger? You laugh at the suggestion. Why not laugh equally when those whom you love have passed on, not to New York, or Chicago, or London, but in the presence of God?

I do not ask that you should open a door into your souls through which all who feel disposed on this side should enter in to possess it. You can, if you like, either on this side or that, enter into companionship with the good or the bad. And I dare say that it is as true, on this side as on yours, that there is a possibility of making acquaintances who may be difficult to shake off. But so it is in London. You do not shrink from coming up to London from the country because in London there are many thousands of thieves, drunkards, swindlers, and men of evil and vicious life.

THE SAME YET NOT THE SAME

All is so new, and there are such unexpected samenesses as well as differences. When, for instance, we wake into the new life we are still in the same world. There are all the familiar things around us—the walls, the pictures, the window, the bed, and the only new things is your own body out of which you stand and wonder how it can be that it is there, and that it is no longer you. And then you begin clearly to understand what has happened. It is very much like experiences you have in dreams, which, after all, are often due to the same cause, the conscious soul leaving the physical frame, which, however, remains breathing. The first thing you notice that is not the same is the Angel. You are the same. I mean that there is no break in your consciousness, your memory, your sex. I was woman in my bodily life, and I am woman still. There is no change there. But you are in a manner different.

A FLIGHT THROUGH SPACE

We went through space at a great speed. I did not feel the speed so much while in motion as when we stayed and discovered how fast and how far we had come. When we stayed it was not in this world at all. We had left your planet and were now speeding through space. I was hardly conscious of movement. We went as we think. Only the things we saw at first disappeared, and there was nothing to check or time our flight. We were together, my Guide and I. We went to a place at a great distance from your earth. The distance I cannot measure. Nor do we take account of distance, when you have only to think to be anywhere. The stars and the worlds, of which you see gleaming twinklings at night, are to us all as familiar as the village-home to a villager. We can go where we please, and we do please very often.

William T. Stead writing, perhaps more notes from spirits. Portrait by E. H. Mills, 1905. (Public domain.)

THE BLUE ISLAND: EXPERIENCES OF A NEW ARRIVAL BEYOND THE VEIL

CHAPTER I: THE ARRIVAL

MANY years ago I was attracted by an article published on a newly-issued book on the subject of spirit communication, and after reading the book carefully several times, I was forced to admit its soundness. I was struck by the plain and practical ideas of the writer. That book was the first cause of my becoming actively interested in this big and amazing work. From that time onward I did all in my power to prove and then forward the movement. Many people know this; and those who do not can become acquainted with the details if they wish. Therefore I am going to pass at once from my first earth interest in the occult to my first occult interest in the earth.

Just as I was overcome with astonishment and satisfaction on first reaching conviction on earth, so I was astonished almost equally on my coming to this land and finding that my knowledge of this subject gained on earth was strikingly correct in nearly all the chief points. There was a great satisfaction in proving this. I was at once amazed and delighted to find so much truth in all I had learnt: for although I had believed implicitly, I was not entirely without grave misgivings upon many minor details. Hence my general satisfaction when I recognised things and features which, though I had accepted whilst on earth, I had scarcely anticipated would be as I now found them. This must sound somewhat contradictory, but I want you to understand that my earthly misgivings were based on the fear that perhaps the spirit world had a formula of its own which was quite different to our earth mentality, and that, therefore, the many points were transmitted to us in such a form and in such expression as we on earth would be able to grasp and appreciate, and were not in themselves the precise descriptions, owing to the limitations of earth word-expression.

Of my actual passing from earth to spirit life I do not wish to write more than a few lines. I have already spoken of it several times and in several places. The first part of it was naturally an extremely discordant one, but from the time my physical life was ended there was no longer that sense of struggling with overwhelming odds; but I do not wish to speak of that.

My first surprise came when—I now understand that to your way of thinking I was then dead—I found I was in a position to help people. From being in dire straits myself, to being able to lend a hand to others, was such a sudden transition that I was frankly and blankly surprised. I was so taken aback that I did not consider the why and the wherefore at all. I was suddenly able to help. I knew not how or why and did not attempt to enquire. There was no analysis then; that came a little later.

I was also surprised to find a number of friends with me, people I knew had passed over years before. That was the first cause of my realising the change had taken place. I knew it suddenly and was a trifle alarmed. Practically instantaneously I found myself looking for myself. Just a moment of agitation, momentary only, and then the full and glorious realisation that all I had learnt was true. Oh, how badly I needed a telephone at that moment! I felt I could give the papers some headlines for that evening. That was my first realisation; then came a helplessness—a reaction—a thought of all my own at home—they didn't know yet. What would they think of me? Here was I, with my telephone out of working order for the present. I was still so near the earth that I could see everything going on there. Where I was I could see the wrecked ship, the people, the whole scene; and that seemed to pull me into action—I could help! ... and so in a few seconds—though I am now taking a long time to tell you, it was only a few seconds really—I found myself changed from the helpless state to one of action; helpful not helpless—I was helpful, too, I think.

I pass a little now. The end came and it was all finished with. It was like waiting for a liner to sail; we waited until all were aboard. I mean we waited until the disaster was complete. The saved—saved; the dead—alive. Then in one whole we moved our scene. It was a strange method of traveling for us all, and we were a strange crew, bound for we knew not where. The whole scene was indescribably pathetic. Many, knowing what had occurred, were in agony of doubt as to their people left behind and as to their own future state. What would it hold for them? Would they be taken to see Him? What would their sentence be? Others were almost mental wrecks. They knew nothing, they seemed to be uninterested in everything, their minds were paralysed. A strange crew indeed, of human souls waiting their ratings in the new land.

A matter of a few minutes in time only, and here were hundreds of bodies floating in the water—dead—hundreds of souls carried through the air, alive; very much alive, some were. Many, realising their death had come, were enraged at their own powerlessness to save their valuables. They fought to save what they had on earth prized so much.

The scene on the boat at the time of striking was not pleasant, but it was as nothing to the scene among the poor souls newly thrust out of their bodies, all unwillingly. It was both heartbreaking and repellent. And thus we waited—waited until all were collected, until all was ready, and then we moved our scene to a different land.

It was a curious journey that. Far more strange than anything I had anticipated. We seemed to rise vertically into the air at terrific speed. As a whole we moved, as if we were on a very large platform, and this was hurled into the air with gigantic strength and speed, yet there was no feeling of insecurity ... We were quite steady. I cannot tell how long our journey lasted, nor how far from the earth we were when we arrived, but it was a gloriously beautiful arrival. It was like walking from your own English winter gloom into the radiance of an Indian sky. There, all was brightness and beauty. We saw this land far off when we were approaching, and those of us who could understand realised that we were being taken to the place destined for all those people who pass over suddenly—on account of its general appeal. It helps the nerve-racked newcomer to fall into line and regain mental balance very quickly. We arrived feeling, in a sense, proud of ourselves. It was all lightness, brightness. Everything as physical and quite as material in every way as the world we had just finished with.

Our arrival was greeted by welcomes from many old friends and relations who had been dear to each one of us in our earth life. And having arrived, we people who had come over from that ill-fated ship parted company. We were free agents again, though each one of us was in the company of some personal friend who had been over here a long while.

CHAPTER II: THE BLUE ISLAND

I HAVE told you a little about the journey and arrival, and I want now to tell you my first impression and a few experiences. I must begin by saying I do not know how long after the collision these experiences took place. It seemed to be a continuation without any break, but I cannot be certain that this was so.

I found myself in company with two old friends, one of them my father. He came to be with me, to help and generally show me round. It was like nothing else so much as merely arriving in a foreign country and having a chum to go around with. That was the principal sensation. The scene from which we had so lately come was already well relegated to the past. Having accepted the change of death, all the horror of our late experience had gone. It might have been fifty years ago instead of, perhaps, only last night. Consequently our pleasure in the new land was not marred by grief at being parted from earth friends. I will not say that none were unhappy, many were; but that was because they did not understand the nearness of the two worlds; they did not know what was possible, but to those who understood the possibilities, it was in a sense the feeling, "Let us enjoy a little of this new land before mailing our news home"; therefore there was little grief on our arrival.

In writing my first experiences I am going to give a certain amount of detail. My old sense of humour is still with me, I am glad to say, and I know that what I have to say now will cause a certain amount of amusement to those who treat this subject lightly, but that I do not mind. I am glad they will find something to smile at—it will make an impression on them that way, and then when their own time comes for the change they will recognise themselves amongst the conditions of which I am going to write. Therefore to that kind of sceptic I just say, "It's all right, friend," and, "You give no offence."

My father and I, with my friend also, set out immediately. A curious thing struck me. I was clothed exactly as I had been, and it seemed a little strange to me to think I had brought my clothing with me! There's number one, Mr. Sceptic!

My father was also dressed as I had always known him. Everything and everybody appeared to be quite normal—quite as on earth.

We went out together and had refreshment at once, and, naturally, that was followed by much discussion about our mutual friends on both sides. I was able to give them news and they gave me information about our friends and also about the conditions ruling in this new country.

Another thing which struck me was the general colouring of the place; of England it would be difficult to say what the impression of colouring is, but I suppose it would be considered grey-green. Here there was no uncertainty about the impression; it was undoubtedly a blue which predominated. A light shade of a deep blue. I do not mean the people, trees, houses, etc., etc., were all blue; but the general impression was that of a blue land.

I commented upon this to my father—who by the way, was considerably more active and younger than he was at time of death, we looked more like brothers. I spoke of this impression of blue, and he explained that it was so in a sense. There was a great predominance of blue rays in the light, and that was why it was so wonderful a place for mental recovery. Now some say, "How completely foolish!" Well, have you not on earth certain places considered especially good for this or that ailment? ... Then bring common-sense to bear, and realise that the next step after death is only a very little one. You do not go from indifferent manhood to perfect godliness! It is not like that; it is all progress and evolution, and as with people, so with lands. The next world is only a complement of your present one.

We were a quaint population in that country. There were people of all conditions, of all colours, all races and all sizes: all went about freely together, but there was a great sense of caring only for oneself, self-absorption. A bad thing on earth, but a necessary thing here, both for the general and individual good. There would be no progress or recovery in this land without it, as a result of this absorption there was a general peace amongst these many people, and this peace would not have been attained without this self-centredness. No one took notice of any other. Each stood for himself, and was almost unaware of all the others.

There were not many people whom I knew. Most of those who came to meet me had disappeared again, and I saw scarcely any I knew, except my two companions. I was not sorry for this. It gave me more chance of appreciating all this new scene before me. There was the sea where we were, and I and my companions went for a long walk together along the shore. It was not like one of your seaside resorts, with promenade and band; it was a peaceful and lovely spot. There were some very big buildings on our right and on our left was the sea. All was light and bright, and again this blue atmosphere was very marked. I do not know how far we went, but we talked incessantly of our new conditions and of my own folk at home and of the possibility of letting them know how it fared with me, and I think we must have gone a long way. If you can imagine what your world would look like if it were compressed into a place, say, the size of England—with some of all people, all climates, all scenery, all buildings, all animals—then you can, perhaps, form an idea of this place I was in. It must all sound very unreal and dreamlike, but believe me, it was only like being in a foreign country and nothing else, except that it was absorbingly interesting.

I want to give you a picture of this new land without going too deeply into the minute details. We arrived at length at a huge building, circular and with a great dome. Its general appearance was of a dome only—on legs—I mean a great dome supported on vast columns, circular and very big. This again, in the interior, was an amazingly lovely blue. It was not a fantastic structure in any way. It was just a beautiful building, as you have on earth—do not imagine anything fairylike; it was not. This blue was again very predominant, and it gave me a feeling of energy. I wanted immediately to write. I would like to have been a poet at that moment, but as it was I just wanted to express myself with pen and ink.

We stayed there some time and had refreshment very similar, it seemed to me, to what I had always known, only there was no flesh food. Everything appeared quite normal there, too, and the absence of some things which would on earth have been present was not noticed. The curious thing was that the meal did not seem at all a necessity—it was there, and we all partook of it lightly, but it was more from habit than need—I seemed to draw much more strength and energy out of the atmosphere itself. This I attributed to the colour and air. It was while we were in this place that my father explained the reason and work of the different buildings I had noted on our walk together.

CHAPTER III: INTERESTING BUILDINGS

LOOKED upon as a meal—a lunch out—it was the longest one I have ever known and without question the most interesting. I learnt a great deal in those first few hours with my father. It was all conversational, but it was of great use to me and of vast interest. He explained to me that the place we were then in was a temporary rest house, one of many, but the one most used by newly-arrived spirit people. It was nearest to earth conditions and was used because it resembled an earth place in appearance. There were other buildings used for the same purpose as well as for other purposes; by that I mean there is more than one of each.

These different houses were not all alike, they varied considerably in outward appearance, but there is no need to describe each. To call it a big building is sufficient, and by that you must understand a place like your museum or your portrait gallery, or your large hotels ... anything you like, and it is near enough. But it was not fantastic in any way and had no peculiarities, therefore by "building" I mean a building only.

There were a great number of these places in different parts— not grouped together, but variously placed about this land.

It seems that all the senses are provided for here. The chief work on this island is to get rid of unhappiness at parting from earth ties, and therefore, for the time being, the individual is allowed to indulge in most of earth's pleasures. There are attractions of all kinds to stimulate and generally to tone up strength. Whatever the person's particular interest on earth has been, he can follow it up and indulge in it here also for the present. All mental interests and almost all physical interests can be continued here, for that one reason of coaxing the newcomer to a level mental outlook.

There are houses given over to book study, music, to athleticism of all kinds. Every kind of physical game can be practised—you can ride on horseback, you can swim in the sea. You can have all and any kind of sport which does not involve the taking of life. In a minor degree that can be had too, but not in reality; that is only a make-believe.

From this you will understand that particular buildings are given over to their own kind of work. The man who has spent his life in games, heart and soul, would be disconsolate without them here ... he can have them and enjoy them to the full; but he will find that after a time the desire is not so keen and he will turn to other interests automatically, though gradually, and it may be that he will never entirely abandon his games, but the desire will be less absorbing. On the other hand, the man who used his life for, say, music, for instance, will find his desire, his interest and his ability increasing by leaps and bounds—because music belongs to this land. He will find that by spending much time in one of the music houses, as he will if his life is music, his knowledge and ability are amazingly increased. Then there is the bookworm. He, too, finds intense satisfaction in his new-found facilities. Knowledge is unlimited—works of priceless value, lost upon earth, are in existence here. He is provided for.

The keen business man on earth whose only interest is in making his business successful will also find scope for his ability. He will come in contact with the house of organisation, and he will find himself linked up with work transcending in interest anything that he could have imagined for himself whilst upon earth.

Now all this is done for a reason. Everyone is provided for. On arriving here there is often much grief; grief that is sometimes incapacitating, and no movement forward can be made until the individual wishes it himself. Progress cannot be forced upon him. Thus in the scheme of creation the blessed Creator has devised this wonderful means of appealing to the main interest on earth of each one. Everyone comes in touch with the chief longing of earth life, and is given opportunity to indulge in it, and thus progress is assured.

In all things that are purely and solely of the earth, the interest flags after a little time; a reaction, a gradual process—nothing is dramatic here—and the person passes from this to another interest which on earth would be called a mental one. Those whose interests have been in this mind-category will continue and enlarge the scope of their work, and will progress along the same lines—the others change.

Whilst in this Blue Island each one is very much in touch with the conditions left behind. At first there is nothing done but what is both helpful and comforting later there is a refining process to be gone through. At first it is possible to be closely in touch with the home left behind, but after a little time there is a reaction from this desire to be so close to earth, and when that sets in the process of eliminating earth and flesh instincts begins. In each case this takes a different course, a different length of time.

In trying thus to explain the uses of this land and its buildings, I have not numbered them "Building A" for so-and-so, "Building B" for this, that and the other, but, in a conversational way, I hope I have helped you to understand and form a general idea of this country and some of its conditions. I hope I have made it clear how, after a time, the desire for earth things leaves us all. It may be a short or long time, according to the disposition of the person concerned. Take the athlete. He loves his games, his running, his physical strength and his muscular exercise. Well, he will love it here as much. He will love it here more, because he will find an added pleasure in feeling no fatigue, a sharpened enjoyment altogether, but after a time his appreciation of all this will change. He will not dislike this hitherto loved sport, but he will pass to a different form of it. A form which is full of movement and satisfaction but not a physical affair at all; his mind will become more awake, and he will get enormous mental satisfaction from the studies which will come before him concerning the ways and means of travel here. Locomotion of all kinds here is very different to that which obtains in earth conditions, and this former athlete of earth will drop into line in his new surroundings and will presently realise that life here is a different thing for him, for, though still on the same lines, it holds an increased mental interest. Is that clear? ... Well, apply it in the same fashion to every other type of individual.

CHAPTER IV: LIFE ON THE ISLAND

HAVING given you a little idea of this land and its appearance, I want to tell you about the life of the people here, so that you can form a mental picture in completeness. It is only natural that many should say, "What are they all doing?" Now, this is a very broad question to answer, and to help you to see how big a thing I am dealing with in thus attempting to give my story of the next life, I must put a simple question to you.

I want you to try and imagine you have not been living on earth and that, knowing nothing of earth life, you have suddenly been landed by an airship in the busiest part of the city of London—with all its traffic and its people. You have arrived from some other world and have not seen this sight before. You will exclaim, "How strange! What are they all doing?" Well, could you answer that question easily? It would not mean much to you to be told they are going about their own individual business—one man bakes bread, another sweeps the streets, another drives a cart, and another sits in an office and runs a business—all that would leave you none the wiser. These are facts, and yet you would not understand them. You could not comprehend them. That is my difficulty in trying to make you understand in a satisfactory way the life of this Blue Isle. I have to consider how to explain it. It is no use my telling you that one person sits by the sea all the time, weeping because of her parting from her lover, and another is in a mental stupor from drink, and another still thinks he is ringing the bells of his local chapel on Sunday, etc., etc.—that is not the life, those are only bits of it. Atoms of the whole. I do not want to particularise, I want to generalise, with some detail. Therefore I must say that if you were to pay this land a visit in your earth bodies, as you are at present, you would be struck by the lack of excitement. You would think it all so like earth. That is what you would say to people on your return. "Oh, it's so much like our life here, only there are such a lot of different races of mankind there."

Everyday life for the individual is strikingly like the everyday life he's always been used to. At first he takes a great deal of rest, having the earth habit of sleep—and it is a necessity—he needs sleep here too, for the present. We have no night as you have, but he sleeps and rests just the same. He has his interests in visiting different parts, in exploring the land and its buildings and in studying its animal and vegetable life. He has friends to seek out and to see. He has his pastimes to indulge. He has his new-found desire for knowledge to feed.

The routine of a day here is similar to the routine of a day on earth; the difference being that earth's routine is often made by force of circumstance, whereas here it is made according to the desire for knowledge on this or that subject.

In clothing, we are all practically as on earth and as there are so many races here you can well understand the general appearance of this land is most unusual, and in an odd way particularly interesting and amusing, also instructive. I think I have said that in general appearance we all are as we all were. We are only a very little way from earth, and consequently up to this time we have not thrown off earth ideas. We have gained some new ones, but have as yet discarded few or none.

The process of discarding is a gradual one. As we live here we gain knowledge of many kinds, and come to find so many things, hitherto thought essential, not only of no importance but something of a bore, a nuisance, and that is how we grow to a state of dropping all earth habits. We get to the state of not desiring a smoke, not because we can't have it, or think it not right, but because the desire for it is not there. As with a smoke, so with food, so with many a dozen things; we are just as satisfied without them. We do not miss them; if we did we should have them, and we do have them until the desire is no longer there.

At first there is practical freedom of thought and action, and there are only certain limitations imposed—not by rule but by conditions. Beyond these limitations there is absolute freedom. After a time, when the spirit has advanced to the point of desiring knowledge and enlightenment, he will be drawn like a piece of steel to a magnet, into contact with this or that house of organisation dealing with the subject on which he desires knowledge. From the time of coming into touch with this house the spirit will be, as it were, "at school." He will perforce have to attend this house for instruction. He will spend a good deal of his time there learning, and, when finished with one house, will pass to another, but it is not compulsory information, it is craved-for information, and nothing is given until asked for. You are not forced to acquire anything. You are more than ever free agents. That is why on earth it is so essential to control your bodies by your minds, and not the reverse. When you come here your mind is all-powerful, and everything depends, for your own degree of happiness here, upon the kind of mind you bring with you.

The presence or absence of contentment is entirely due to the earth life you have led, the character formed, opportunities taken and lost, the motive of and for your actions, the help given, the manner of use of help received, your mental outlook and your use and abuse of flesh power. To sum all these up, it is the quality of mind control over body versus body over mind. Mind matters and body matters—on earth. Here only the mind matters, it is in your keeping entirely, and is in whatever state you have made it by your life. On your arrival here the degree of your happiness will be determined automatically by the demands of your mind.

When you are inclined to ask, "What are they all doing there?" turn your mind to some dear one on earth who has taken up an out-of-the-way kind of life somewhere abroad, where you are not in constant and intimate touch, and say of him, "I wonder what he's doing now."... Then answer it yourself by saying, "I suppose he's carrying on." So are we, we people in the Blue Island.

THE

NEXT WORLD

INTERVIEWED

BY

MRS. S. G. HORN

AUTHOR OF "STRANGE VISITORS"

"And often, from that other world on this
Some gleams from great souls gone before may shine."
—J. RUSSELL LOWELL.

CHICAGO:
THE PROGRESSIVE THINKER PUBLISHING HOUSE.
No. 40 Loomis Street.
1896.

THE NEXT WORLD INTERVIEWED

Mrs. S. G. Horn's The Next World Interviewed *presents messages from many notable spirits, several of whom you'll hear from in the next section. In the following pages you'll find out the supposed truth of evolution from Jean Louis Rodolphe Agassiz, a Swiss biologist and geologist, and a professor of Earth's natural history. However, he was also resistant to Darwin's theory, instead choosing to believe in creationism. Agassiz died on December 14, 1873, but spoke from the all-knowing spirit world to share his discoveries about the extraterrestrial origin of humankind.*

Ancient Greek historian, Herodotus, also enlightened readers with tales of a pre-historic race of man. According to Horn, he was among the first spirits to contribute to her book—and one she had "no expectation" of hearing from. "The information communicated by the spirit was as startling and unanticipated as his visit," she added.

PROF. AGASSIZ ON EVOLUTION

I COME from my island home at the call of science, hoping to add something to the information already obtained.

This lady, blindfolded and mesmerised, is rendered sensitive to invisible forces, and in this condition her soul is capable of travelling through space, and taking cognizance of strange unaccredited facts that are transpiring outside of this terrestrial plane of existence.

When restored to her natural condition, the knowledge thus obtained appears to her vague and indistinct, and even while entranced it is difficult for her to perfectly describe what she sees, or to repeat with adequate language what is told her.

This condition of affairs must be borne in mind by my reader in endeavouring to understand the subject of which I treat.

It is but recently that science has been able to trace the record of your globe and the inhabitants thereof; you perceive therefore, if it is difficult to obtain a knowledge of the world on which you live, it must be infinitely more difficult to obtain information of a region so remote as the world which I inhabit.

Geologists will tell you of mammoth animals that lived on the earth centuries ago, and from the beds of rivers dried up and silent for ever, they gather the mighty fragments and fossilised bones of the fauna of a by-gone geological period, and articulate those immense carcases so that they stand before the spectator, strange, inconceivable forms, repulsive and demon-like to the eye unfamiliar with such creations, while they were familiar enough to the beings who lived coeval with their existence. As on your world there have been beings who would appear grotesque and almost impossible creations to the eye of to-day, so on every earth there has been a series of similar evolutions prior to man's taking up his abode thereon.

Man being the perfection of animal form (whose origin is the source of acute investigation by archaeologists and geologists), whose moral and mental faculties place him far above the lower animals, causes a break in the development theory which puzzles the astutest mind of the New School.

My investigations since I have become an inhabitant of this superior world have satisfied me that man originally migrated to earth from a superior planet.

Of his migratory character and the tendency of a higher race to assimilate and fraternise with a lower one, you have a corroborative truth in the rise and fall of nations on earth with their attendant results.

At a remote period this globe was surrounded by an atmosphere very different from that of to-day, and the present race of men could not have existed. During this period to which I allude, earth was visited by beings from a spirit-world, drawn hither by a force of magnetic attraction, which then was a powerful agent, of whose force science gives but a faint idea to the student of Nature.

Influenced by this force, and the spirit of adventure, and by the migratory habit which is co-existent with Nature, this colony of spirits visited your earth. They were men and women of giant-like structure, and they settled on a portion of land which was submerged through the subsequent convulsions of Nature.

The offspring of these beings deteriorated in size, and became more material than their parents by a process of acclimatisation. As I have stated, it was owing to a peculiar condition of earth and atmosphere, that these spiritual beings were able to take up a physical abode upon the earth. In order to understand this statement of fact, the reader must bear in mind that what is called spiritual and immaterial is merely a refined attribute of matter. That electricity, magnetism, and the Od force* are the components of spirit, and are in reality refined material forces, and that spirit and matter are identical, yet differing as heat differs from cold, and light differs from opacity.

These beings, as I term them, were of different grades of perfection. The most highly developed among them brought a taste for music, sculpture, and painting, and a love for beautiful and graceful forms, of which their descendants in ancient Egypt and Greece have left mementos.

As I have said, these beings (who, in the present atmosphere, would be unseen by a mortal's eye upon the earth), drew around them a material covering, and as man now throws off every seven years the outer form, supplying its place with new material, so they gathered to themselves from surrounding elements corporeal forms, which, however, they in time relinquished.

The existence of the first race of men was of a much longer duration than that of the present inhabitants of earth. The physical forms in each succeeding generation, while deteriorating, became less adapted to the necessities of the spirit; and now it is only by the aid of science and the constant application of inventions to the wants of the body, that to-day man's spirit is able to preserve its existence within its present frail tenement.

It is impossible to go back to the origin of life, because it is of eternity; and I believe candidly myself, that there has been no beginning.

I know that there are worlds in existence more numerous than the sands on the sea shore, and an eternity could not number them. These worlds are peopled with beings possessing moral and spiritual powers. They have various degrees of skill and natural ability: some superior to those of the inhabitants of earth, and others inferior. These beings live on for ever in different degrees of sublimation; and as the winged seed which is borne along the air bears its fructifying life to a distant soil, so in the superior world spiritual inhabitants are carried by magnetic and electric forces to people distant worlds.

The comet, that strange visitant, carries in its brilliant flying chariot, spirits on the same mission through space.

I apprehend that what now seems obscure to scientists will be deciphered and made clear by future investigations in the science of magnetism and Spiritualism. From my home here above the clouds, on this beautiful island where I pursue my studies, I watch with deep interest the investigations of such men as Wallace, Tyndall, Crookes, Lubbock, and the large coterie of English students, and their brethren in America and in other parts of the world.

---

*The "Od force" refers to subtle emanations that come from all forms of matter, from the stars to us mortals, and are perceived only by the truly sensitive. The term comes from "odic force," first introduced in 1858 by Baron Karl von Reichenbach, a German chemist, geologist, naturalist, and philosopher.

HERODOTUS DISCUSSES A PRE-HISTORIC RACE OF MAN

THE race of Europeans upon the earth at the present day are pleased to date back 1800 years, and look upon that short period of time as a point remote in history. Eighteen hundred years back of that is lost in the labyrinth of tradition. Six thousand years has been accredited as the period of the earth's existence, and Bible historians have built up a form of theology upon their supposed data.

Thousands of years before Cheops trod upon the earth, ere Ramesis the Great sat upon his throne, centuries before the supposed period of creation, there lived upon the earth a great nation—a people skilled in art and science.

They were tall in stature with regular features, in appearance between the ancient Greek and Egyptian; they believed in the immortality of the soul, and traced their origin to the gods.

The walls of their great cities are buried beneath the sea. Their temples and monuments are washed by the sands of the ocean. The face of the globe has changed since that day. Great continents have been formed, and the eastern and western hemispheres are divided as they were not at that era.

In the far past, the Spirit-world in its revolution entered into the atmosphere of the material world, and beings from the World of Spirits came upon the earth and dwelt bodily, and brought with them their creative genius, and thus was founded these lost cities.

These inhabitants of a rarefied world brought with them their poetry, their arts and sciences, and man ascended from the animal state, to a mental and emotional one.

The scientific explorers of the present day are tracing man's footsteps from a lower to a higher state of being, but they have yet failed to trace the evolution of the soul from the forces of Nature. The immortal spark which made man the great being that he has proved himself to be in the past—where in Egypt, Syria, Nineveh, and India, and Greece, and the islands of the sea, he has left wonderful tokens of the creative power of the soul—is not an evolution from the lowest germ of matter, but a spark from the great Creative Mind. The humblest animal or bird upon the earth has its brain and nerve connections thereto, which form a battery, and, acted upon by the sun and heat, produces life—motion.

That we call animal life, the life which man possesses in common with the lowest forms of creation. But there is another life, a spiritual life, quickened by a spiritual sun, which animates man, who is the highest form of creation.

The pyramids of Egypt, the object of whose erection has remained a mystery to man, were constructed, for the purpose of communicating with spirits, by the ancestors of these remote people I have spoken of. The great mystery of communicating with spiritual beings by mesmeric passes, and resorting to high mounds or elevations for this intercourse, was a secret in the hands of a few mediumistic and enlightened priests and nobles of that day. Among them the laws of chemical affinities, and the use of certain gases, unknown to-day, and of so-called mesmeric influences, were understood and applied for the purpose of communicating with the Unseen World (but under these conditions it was seen). The mass of men were mere animals, and this science was known only to the learned classes; the mysterious power of communicating with the supernatural world had the effect of stimulating the faculties, and increasing the knowledge, and awakening the higher emotions, and love of the beautiful, even among the uninitiated.

Temples of immense size were erected towering far into the clouds, as a magnet to draw the favourite spirit to that point. All ancient and classic history (so-called) is replete with accounts of spirits appearing to men. In my day it was of such frequent occurrence that no surprise was awakened by it, but the people of whom I speak lived in daily association with the Spirit-world.

All the earlier races of men held belief in pre-existence, and that gods could come down and take possession of the forms of men. The earliest Hebrew records are replete with traditions that angels and gods descended in bodily form, and ate, and talked, and walked, with the patriarchs of old. Long before the days of the Jewish priesthood, spirits walked upon the earth, and intermarried with the inhabitants of earth.

Only among certain races of peculiar physiological development could this advent from the Spirit-world take place.

The ancient Greeks were particularly indebted to the inhabitants of the Spirit-world. Mount Olympus was truly the seat of the gods, as Mount Sinai became in later days the seat or throne of Jehovah. All high mounds are more accessible to spirits. Being lifted from the lower strata of the earth's atmosphere, they are better adapted to the sublimated condition of spiritual visitants.

PHENEAS SPEAKS

DIRECT SPIRIT COMMUNICATIONS
IN THE FAMILY CIRCLE
REPORTED BY

ARTHUR CONAN DOYLE, M.D., LL.D.

NO COPYRIGHT
(U.S.A. EXCEPTED)

THE PSYCHIC PRESS AND BOOKSHOP
ABBEY HOUSE, VICTORIA STREET, S.W.
Tel.: Franklin 6248

TRADE AGENTS:
SIMPKIN, MARSHALL, HAMILTON, KENT AND CO., LTD.,
STATIONERS' HALL, E.C. 4

PHENEAS SPEAKS

Sir Arthur Conan Doyle's zeal for Spiritualism is mentioned in the introduction to this book, as is his wife Jean's mediumship. Among the spirits she channeled was an ancient Arabian from a Mesopotamian city called Ur. His name was Pheneas, and he claimed to have lived before the time of Abraham. This old spirit was in touch often with the Doyles during the mid 1920s. "Say just 'Pheneas' and I will come quicker than if you said a number on the telephone," he told them, as if he was their own personal genie.

Pheneas gave business advice, suggested travel dates for the couple, and even helped them find a new home in a region of Southern England called the New Forest. "It is a wonderful place," he said in May of 1924. "The atmosphere is perfect."

He also liked predicting doom and gloom for the world. More specifically, the ancient man from Ur predicted doom for Doyle's friend and non-believer, Houdini. On April 12, 1925, Pheneas told Jean, "Houdini is doomed, doomed, doomed. He will not be allowed to stand in the way of God's progress." The great magician died just over a year later, on October 31, 1926.

Doyle collected all these messages into a book, Pheneas Speaks, *in 1927. A few delightful excerpts regarding evil, hope, and vegetarianism follow.*

"THE GREATEST THING THAT COULD POSSIBLY HAPPEN FOR HUMANITY"

July 5, 1924—When the great change comes to humanity then all creeds and churches will cease to exist or the people of all nations will realise how they have utterly failed them in their hour of need. All, all, every colour and sect and nation will turn to spiritualism, and so the world will be changed and the shams will be swept away for ever. Then comes the Millennium. When you come over here to the land of your dreams you will find that only love prevails, and the sun shines, and all, all is beautiful, and the heart is never hurt. From here you will see the progress of the world under the new conditions, it will all be most interesting and wonderful to behold. The crop is nearly due, the seeds are almost all in, the rain is now to come, and then the sunshine. It is the greatest thing that could possibly happen for humanity.

"THE RUBBISH HEAP OF HUMANITY"

April 12, 1925—I would like to—please I want to say this. The people are struggling against a force that is crushing them, and a pit of evil has been growing deeper and deeper in the world, and its forces have been dragging down humanity. So we have made a central battery to prevent the destruction of mankind. There are pits covered with beautiful green that seem safe to walk on, but they are fatal. That is why we must interfere, to cut out those dangers for mankind.

You understand it is just like a microbe in the body—a little, wee thing, but centres grow and grow till the whole beautiful body is destroyed, and is not as God made it. So with the human race.

Much has to be swept away with the rubbish heap of humanity. It is like the ashes you put on soil to do it good. Those experiences will be a living memory of what to avoid in the newborn earth, where Love will prevail in days to come, tenderness, simplicity, and the fulfillment of all that God meant humanity to be.

… We are at present meeting continually, first to discuss the reports from those who have certain tasks upon the earth, secondly to send out to the centres instructions respecting the latest developments in the chemical world from here to the earth plane. Our people have been to study the conditions in different parts of the world. They have readjusted every mechanism. This has been circulated round to those who deal with the various districts— this is done from our Central Committee. Then there are those who report on the evil forces on their plane; then there is above that the great power descending from a very high sphere, with instructions to all as to what each unit is to do, and prepare for. The receiving stations in the homeland have to be ready. Then above that are wonderful messages of inspiration, coming to revitalise all of us, so that we may be channels of His great light to descend upon earth, and to the intermediary spheres, like a battery of electricity.

… After a time dawn will come—a new sun will shine forth—a sun that has more warmth and health in it.

The earth will grow green once more. The flowers will appear. Humanity will awaken to a world reborn. The old things will have passed away, and the earth will know them no more.

"SURELY I COULD NOT HAVE LIKED THAT"

April 25, 1925—All is easier on our side than in this moth-eaten, muddy world. This is like a very hideous brown ghost-form of real life, which is much more solid. When we visit it, we say: "Surely I could not have liked that. Don't tell me there was ever a time when I wanted to stay in that. It is inconceivable."

We have all you have, without the shadows. All the best you have is intensified with us. All the beauty, but no ugly human elements. No selfishness, no anger, nothing ugly. Only beauty.

You will meet all who have love and sympathy for you.

If you do your simple duty as God means you to do it in your daily life, you will be in this beautiful place.

"HUMANITY WILL SOON BE STAGGERED"

March 25, 1926—In a little time there will be a great discovery of an electric nature made by spirit power by a man who knows nothing of electricity. It will mean seeing and hearing by means of electricity.

This spiritual knowledge is coming into your world in little rills all from a source which is inexhaustible. Soon these rills will unite and form pools and lakes, which will submerge everything.

Conditions are mixed to-night. There have been workmen and others in this room who have mixed the atmosphere.

You must understand the difficulties. Electricity is as coarse as lead compared to these fine psychic vibrations.

All is well. There is a very great man on our side who will inspire you at your address to-morrow.

Humanity will soon be staggered at the enormous power shown from on high.

The result will be to lower all the bridges of thought in the direction of the spirit world. You Spiritualists will have to get busy, all of you, in helping to lower those bridges, and giving the tickets of entrance to those who would pass over to a greater conception of faith, thought, and knowledge.

A gardener in a conservatory, when he sees a life-killing fly destroying the plants that he lovingly cultured and tended, will spray those plants with an anti-death toxin. So will the great Gardener when He sees His beloved flowers being destroyed by noxious growths. God bless you!

Let your mind be very open to us—to our directions—in the next twenty-four hours. Don't shut the doors and windows. Let us in. Don't get it too tight. You understand.

"WE DON'T HAVE MEAT HERE"

April 26, 1926—We don't have meat here. We love all living creatures because God made them, and He loves all that He has created, for in each there is a spark of God, and that is love—for their mates, their little ones, for something.

I get troubled when I see the creatures sacrificed to the appetite of man. But their days are numbered. Comparatively few more will be sacrificed, because in the new world humanity will have awakened to the sense of the enormity of the action which they take when they absorb a life that God has not done with—I mean when they kill creatures to fill their own bodies.

Your hearts are full of love for the animal world, and you will be glad at the memory that you had sympathy on the dark earth plane.

We see the difficulties of dietetic change—soon you start a new era—you begin life instead of existence. Now you come up to the top story when, for the first time, you will see things as they are. Humanity will be like the worms when they come up to the surface.

"BE ON YOUR GUARD"

August 27, 1926—All is well. The dark forces have set a movement going in order to check God's power, which they see approaching the earth. They will fail.

These forces are evil, and must go. You will be approached soon by letter by another, who will claim to be a Spiritualist, but who plots evil. Be on your guard. We have our eye on him.

There will come much good from a spirit source, a medium, who has been regarded with some suspicion. Tell the Medium when she wakes that the matter she is wondering about will be all right.

She will be wonderful. She has God's great work to do. Tear-dimmed eyes will look up at her, and they will lighten in joy as they see the power that God has given her. So long as she uses those powers no harm can touch any of you.

AFTERLIFESTYLES OF THE RICH AND FAMOUS

AFTERLIFESYLES OF THE RICH AND FAMOUS

What would luminaries such as Shakespeare, Benjamin Franklin, Abraham Lincoln, Mark Twain, Edgar Allan Poe and others say if they could be heard once again? Based on the number of posthumous messages received and printed in spiritualist books, these famous people proved just as popular in the afterlife as they were during their time on Earth. Poe penned new poems and reflections on his own life. Franklin wrote a whole new set of beyond-the-veil aphorisms. Shakespeare granted a full interview, giving new perspectives on his body of work. And Lincoln described life after assassination and offered a few Commander-in-Chief thoughts as World War I raged.

In Strange Visitors *(1869), author Henry J. Horn admits in the introduction that "its title and contents will doubtless at first sight cause a smile of incredulity," and might be thought to "entrap an unsuspecting public into the perusal of a sensational hoax," he explained that anyone familiar with those individuals presented would "readily perceive a marked resemblance in style to that of the authors named."*

These remarkable words were obtained through a clairvoyant who Horn described being in "an abnormal or trance condition and with her eyes closed." As words journeyed from the spirit world through her lips they were transcribed in pencil to be shared with the world.

With celebrities, mediums could go beyond personal messages from lost loved ones and provide dispatches from the beyond that everyone would want to hear. This allowed for more profits, or another way to preach religious beliefs, or both. Just like anyone in business today, they knew celebrity sells.

Mrs. Lincoln photographed with her husband. Photo by William Mumler, as published in Human Nature, *December 1874.*

ABRAHAM LINCOLN

When the sixteenth President of the United States was assassinated in 1865, Spiritualism was as popular as ever. With so many thousands of Civil War casualties, people looked to mediums for comfort and a chance to make contact with their lost loved ones. Lincoln himself was no stranger to Spiritualism. First Lady Mary Todd Lincoln was a practicing Spiritualist and held séances in the White House. It's believed the President attended a few of them. They had hoped to hear from their youngest son, Willie, who passed away in 1862.

Given the Lincolns' interest, the booming Spiritualism market, and of course, the fact that Lincoln was one of the most high-profile people in America, mediums knew people would want to hear anything they could from him. So they gave it to them. In these pages you'll find descriptions of Lincoln's passing into the Other Side, a political warning, and a brief interview.

MY PASSAGE TO SPIRIT-LIFE

IT is scarcely necessary to allude to the manner of my death, as it is well known to the public. The feelings that attended my "taking off" affect me even now. There is something, to the spirit, truly awful in being called from the scene of active life without a moment's warning, without opportunity to bid adieu to friends, to embrace long-tried companions—with not one brief moment afforded, for settling affairs of life and transacting necessary business, before a final departure from the shores of Time. Mine was truly a sublime and awful exit! Not that I was entirely unprepared; I had long felt that a dark cloud overhung my sky, and had forebodings of some strange, undefined calamity awaiting me; I felt it when I entered that theatre at Washington. Some morbidly pious individuals, who undertake to think for the good Lord, have considered my assassination as a judgment upon me for visiting a play-house, but they will discover when they reach *this Port*, as a good clergyman remarked concerning the great disaster at the Brooklyn Theatre, that it matters not if a man leave for his Eternal Home from a theatre or from a church, providing he is prepared for the journey. *I was* prepared, inasmuch as I believed that every public officer should hold his life in his hand, ready to lay it down in the nation's service; and from the moment that it was revealed to me that I was chosen to release the slave from bondage, from that moment I felt that I was foredoomed, and I was willing that my life should be sacrificed for that necessary accomplishment.

On that fatal night which ended with my life's tragedy, when I fell mortally wounded in the theatre, and after a few moments of anguish—a brief time of mental despair followed by unconsciousness—I awakened to find myself a spirit among spirits, and to realise that I was being actually crowned with a wreath of laurels by the hand of Washington, and that I was surrounded by an innumerable company of spirits "which no man could number,"—when I heard the grand vibrations of heavenly music surging through the air, filling my soul with an ecstatic bliss beyond mortal comprehension; then a weight was removed from my heart, and I experienced a happiness that I had not felt for *ten long years!*

Spirits of the Next World are intimately connected with mortals, how intimately I never realised until I became a denizen of the Summer-land. Then I found that the inhabitants of that shadowy realm were perfectly familiar with my life, and under the direction of a wise power they had raised me from obscurity, and had elected me to be the Liberator of the Southern slaves. They had foreseen the dangers that encompassed me, and had used every effort to notify me of the plot in preparation to take my life. They had warned me again and again through mediums and my own clairvoyance. They knew the danger, but failed to avert it!

They foresaw also the long train of evils that would follow the emancipation—blighting the fair South, and producing temporary destruction to bring about a future state of progress.

But such is the order of life! The field must be mowed down before it can grow another and better kind of grain. A plantation looks bare and unsightly, when the white cotton is stripped from the pod, and sent off to the looms; but it returns again in the form of a beautiful fabric which will clothe multitudes. So I believe it will be with the South.

She is like the stripped plantation now, but she will receive benefits untold, in the form of renewed energy, and freedom from debasing tyranny.

It shall be no longer *North* and *South*, but one people. The Northerners must help the Southerners build their factories, lay their railroads, and strive in every way to aid them in reconstructing their fallen fortunes.

I wish to say a few words about my wife; it has given me great grief to see her treated as an insane person. Some thought I was not altogether right, because I had peculiar dreams and visions, and sometimes consulted mediums; but I must inform them that those who scoff at these things are more insane than they who believe in them.

It is said, that Spiritualism fills the insane asylums. If any cause could render a woman insane, the distressing events which attended and followed my sudden departure were sufficient to have made my wife so. But her belief in spirit-communion upheld and sustained her, and it was only through a misunderstanding of spirit-direction that she placed herself in a situation whereby she could have such a charge brought against her; but we hastened to her rescue and inspired some receptive noble minds to secure her release from a living tomb.

I do not know that it is necessary for me to speak about the present difficulties of the country, or to applaud General Grant's course, though I heartily do.*

It is impossible to put this country back on its onward march of progress, but bad men will arise now and then and hold office. It is not always possible to judge between a demagogue and a true lover of his country. One who makes the loudest assertions, swears the strongest, and promises the greatest—that one will naturally attract the ignorant. Boys will always turn from the rising sun to look at a bonfire. I remarked while I was in the White House, how much more show was made by the liveried servant than by his master.

Grant, who seems so quiet and befogged behind the smoke of his cigar, is a perfect master of the situation. Do not force him to don the livery and make a harlequin of himself, as he would do if he followed the advice of the thousands who beset him.

A soldier is better with two legs, but if one has been cut off, he had better wear a wooden leg than none at all. The nation has lost one of its legs, the South is trying to take away its wooden one (that is the *black votes*) and make it run on one. I tell you it will not run long.

---

* Delivered while General Grant was filling his last term of office, the winter of 1876-77, Dec. 16.

A WORLD WAR I WARNING

This plate was received by me October, 1917. It was written while lying on a table in the bright sunlight and while no human hand was within five feet from it. It bears mute and unmistakable evidence that it is a message from and in the handwriting of Abraham Lincoln. It reads as follows:

> "Dear Sir: The deadly foe is on our own shores as well as abroad. This country in its drastic action will have to strike the enemy with a double-edged sword, for the common foe is here as well as abroad. The struggle looks like an extended one as to time, but victory comes at the price of vigilance. We can win.
>
> Truly, A. Lincoln."

This communication evidently refers to the European war. It was written while our armies were mobilizing for the conflict and just as the terrible war cloud was overshadowing all American life.

It is predicted by those in the spirit world that forces are now at work, here in America and Canada, which will result in an extended conflict, and cause much blood to be shed after the European war is ended. Whether it is the war between labor and capital or a continuation of the struggle which has shown itself, I am not informed. It is quite likely that "deadly foe" referred to the enemies of our government.

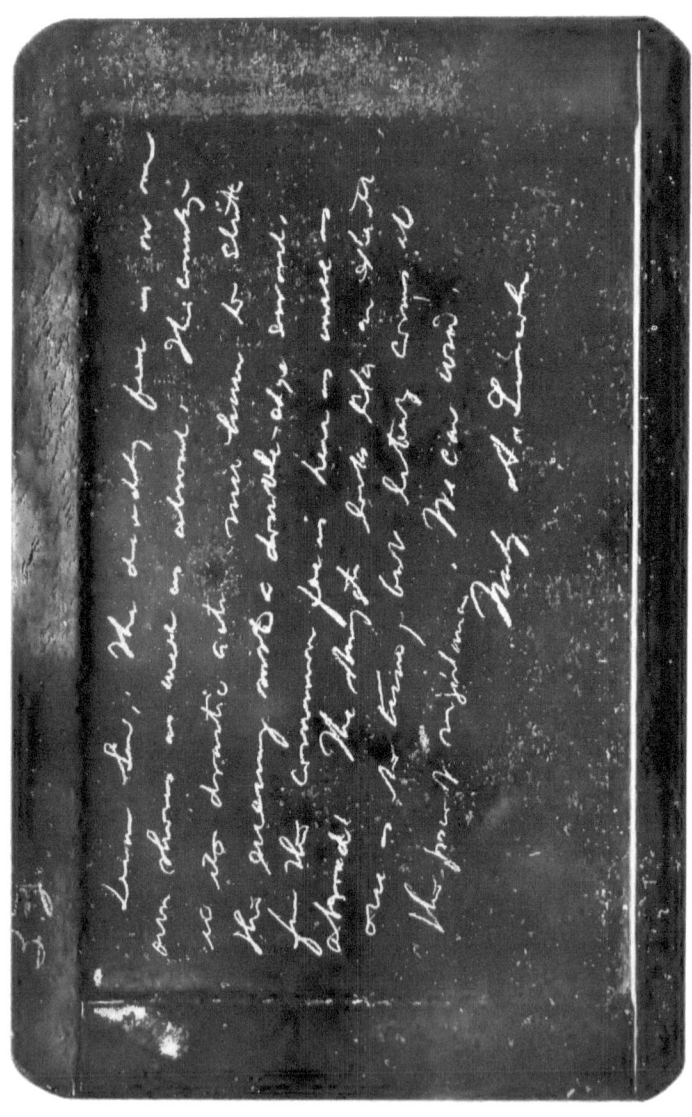

Slate with a message received from Abraham Lincoln in October, 1917. As seen in Photographic Copies of Written Messages From the Spirit World.

AN INTERVIEW

Q.—Do you meet in your new sphere those who were the cause of your death, and if so, with your increased knowledge, do you feel anger or aversion toward them?
A.—Zones of spiritual life are so overlapped and intermixed that those of us who went out from your sphere through blind and bloody ways are so much aware of the sense barriers which shut off the perception of the boundaries between spirit and flesh, that no vengeful feeling can remain even in individual cases.

Q.—Then you bear such persons no ill-will?
A.—Brothers are we all, even Booths.

Q.—If this is Lincoln who replies, tell us in what light you now view Booth's act.
A.—John Wilkes Booth was the ordained man whose maddened brain was used to emphasize the divine way to martyrdom for the sake of the work of life's progress.

Q.—We are then to understand that you are now from your higher point of view content with the manner of your death.
A.—You ask am I content that my life went out as it did. You want to get evidence as to the higher wisdom evolved in my painful going out?

Q.—Yes, we wish you to state your thought in regard to it.
A.—Warfare of all kinds marks life's progress. Soldiers of life are as surely bound to eternal law as earthly soldiers are bound by military discipline.

Q.—Have you yet personally met John Wilkes Booth?
A.—Soul paths diverge, as sense paths do.

Portrait of George Washington by Gilbert Stuart. (Public domain)

GEORGE WASHINGTON

In 1878, a booklet called The Experiences and Opinions of George Washington from Spirit Life *offered just what it promised. This detailed and lengthy account of the afterlife must have tired the hand of the dead president's medium, Mrs. M. J. Upham Hendee. Section 1 of his "experiences" and "opinions" follows, along with Washington's thoughts on government and moving the country forward in the late 1800s, according to other mediums.*

THE
EXPERIENCES AND OPINIONS
OF
GEORGE WASHINGTON
FROM
SPIRIT LIFE.

SAN FRANCISCO:
1878.

EXPERIENCES AND OPINIONS

FRIENDS of earth-life, in coming here to bear my testimony with the hosts of spirit friends, regarding our spiritual home and its natural earth-life condition, gives me great pleasure to be enabled to impart a knowledge of the experiences of one whom you have known as a resident upon your earthly sphere.

Having passed the change called death, I still find myself a living, intelligent being, actually alive to all scenes incident to earth-life, yet comprehending a fuller and happier condition; finding there is no death but the beautiful change called death, to be but the birth of the soul into realms of spiritual unfoldments; where like children born into earthlife, we feel the weakness and strangeness of our situation, not comprehending the wonderful change that has come over us; but being guided and strengthened by our loved ones, who meet us at the gateway to welcome us, yielding, trustingly, lovingly to their protection; becoming strengthened, we learn to adapt ourselves to the conditions surrounding us; thus we gradually become awakened and strengthened, until every fibre of the soul is pulsating with new and wonderful emotions, thrilling with joy to learn that we can still communicate with mortals, and impress them with our presence, and that we still can assist and guide them by our influence and teachings, urging them to honesty and truthfulness here, as passports to a higher and more useful life. I therefore give you my experience of having been ushered into a new and to me incomprehensible state of existence, so unlike my idea of heaven as described to ray earthly vision, that you will not be surprised at my astonishment.

My first awakening into spirit-life was like awakening out of sleep on a bright and lovely morning in June, when the freshness of flowers and the music of birds atune all nature to harmony. I could not understand where I was. I was filled with awe at the appearance and grandeur of the wonderful sublime surroundings. While beholding these things, I seemed to recall the past—to realize that I had passed from earth and must now be in heaven. Can this be, I said to myself; and yet everything is as natural as in earth-life. How strange, how wonderful everything seemed, so like earth that I seem to doubt my senses, and yet I know that I must have changed—must have left the form—for I perceived that I had not the same material body; and remembered also the dear friends weeping over me, bidding me farewell; and said surely this is heaven for which I had so often prayed. But it is not so great a change, for everything is so real and life-like, that I shall be able to comprehend its locality and sphere, and its distance from earth—for it is no longer a visionary heaven, but a real local place. While these strange thoughts were passing through my mind, I seemed to be in a kind of pleasing dream; partly asleep and partly awake. While thus wondering as to my condition, a sweet, bright vision of glorified spirits seemed to approach and arouse me to a greater fullness of my condition and surroundings.

One beautiful, bright spirit came out from the number, and extending her arms, cried: "George, my son, you have come to me, and a mother's arms can again embrace you—can watch over you. You have passed beyond the earthly plane, and are now in spirit spheres. My dear devoted mother, how beautiful she seemed; as natural and real as when in the earth-form. The vision opened, and I beheld many dear earth friends coming near to me; many a one who had passed on before—many a loved one whom I had seen depart to that unknown bourn from whence no traveler returns again to take up the form—but who I find do take form of spirit matter and return to visit their earthly scenes, and hover around the dear ones left on the earth plane.

My first awakening to consciousness of this new life, seemed so truly natural I felt a delightful happiness pervading my being. Those dear angels, whose ministering kindness aroused to consciousness my feeble spirit, gave me full assurance of a continued life in this new phase of being. Truly, a light broke in upon my being, a wonderful change, and yet I lived and held converse with those who had long preceded me. My mother, who was truly my guardian spirit, gave me into the protection of those who should assist in strengthening and arousing my self-sustaining power to become an independent being, to act in the great drama of spirit existence. They took me to the most lovely scenes; scenes that bewildered ray feeble conception, and yet so natural that I could only wonder at its life-like associations.

At this time I felt that I was surrounded by a host of divine beings, but upon looking, I saw many of my dear friends of earth rejoicing at my coming—those who had passed on years gone by, who had almost passed out of my mind, had now come to welcome me to this new home. Aged friends were before me now living pictures of youth and beauty, robed in pure, celestial garments of azure brightness. They had come to welcome me to this bright sphere and bear me on to bright and heavenly knowledge of my present condition.

How my soul swelled with emotion at the thought that all were here in this beautiful world, and no one cast out, but all growing brighter as they become acquainted with the true laws of development.

Truly, my first knowledge was astonishment, delight and wonder at the gorgeous scenery of scintillated light from gorgeous domes above—with flowers whose perfume wrapped me within their folds of sweetness—while beautiful birds of every hue warbled forth their strains of music in such sweet tones of melody that I seemed to lose myself amid so much loveliness and grandeur that I slept.

How long, I have no knowledge. I was awaked by a voice saying, "My son, I wish you to come up higher." Looking up, I saw my mother, and with her a band of angels who I had not seen before.

These were a band of martyrs who had come up through great tribulation, who had fought bravely and had won the crown of knowledge, and often returned to earth to minister to those who were still striving for liberty. They had been with us in our dark and trying moments of sorrow and fear, guiding and directing us through the perilous struggle for freedom, and had inspired many a feeble heart and nerved many a palsied arm to oppose the uplifted blow which was raised to crush out that divine spark of freedom that burned upon the altar of our souls. It was to them who had lived and died for that great boon for which we were then contending, that they had come from their bright home to assist us to gain that freedom here which they saw and felt, but could not gain only through the dissolving elements of the flesh. I stood confounded, and said to them do you tell me then that we can return back to earth and become ministering spirits to those we have left there? Truly, my son said an aged sire, such is the truth, and we have come to you, knowing your sympathy and love for those around you, and your impressibility to become en rapport with such as have kind and generous natures to prepare you for a continuation of the mission you are so well adapted to fill. The love of your countrymen and confidence reposed in you, will enable you to do much good for the advancement of that liberty, that generous, confiding love of brotherly kindness which you so generously manifested while sustaining and upholding them in their great struggle for freedom. Truly this is joy unspeakable to know that I may still be permitted to return to earth and mingle again in the scenes I have loved so well—this is joy indeed. I now understand why heaven is such a beautiful place, and why angels are so happy in it—because they can participate in all that has made life happy; a continuation of blest associations; a continuation of a renewed life to do good and receive good; to be givers and receivers. What a wonderful lesson to the soul, that to be happy we must impart our good gifts to others, that they may be benefitted so as to benefit others again—a divine law of the Almighty; the more we give the more we receive. I perceive the overshadowing wisdom of this great lesson. How did my soul bound with delight to know that I could again be permitted to help the down-trodden and suffering of earth. I was truly blest with such heavenly rays of light breaking in upon my yet infant senses as it were, that I seemed to forget those divine beings who surrounded me, and who quietly took me to a gorgeous home, when again I lost myself in repose.

On awakening from this strengthening sleep, I felt invigorated and refreshed, ready to go forth to new duties, my mind being filled with joy unspeakable at the wonderful developments that were transpiring in this new transition.

Again an angel stood before me, and told me to follow him, as I did so, he wafted me through wondrous scenes of changing life, over mountains, whose majestic slopes and towering heights were grand beyond description, passing through flowery valleys whose running streams and cooling shades invited to repose.

Before us lay a lovely valley, whose bosom was real with sweet-tinted mosses and flowers of every hue. Just as we neared an elevation of gently sloping hills, we beheld grottoes and mansions of pearly brightness, dazzling in the sunlight.

A bright angel, too lovely for description, stepped before us, pointing upwards. We raised our eyes, and beheld a charmed circle above shedding rays of light and beauty around us. She spoke, and then I saw the sweet lineaments of a departed friend, who had passed away long years before—one who had enchained my heart in my early youth, when the brow was clear, and sorrow had not set its seal on my brow of care. She stepped or glided forward, extending her hand, saying, "Welcome, friend, welcome here. I have waited long for you as a dear, friend from my earth-home. That band you see coming are dear friends of our early associations. Your presence has drawn them here to welcome you to this new life; they will take you hither to show you their beautiful sphere, when you have become more awakened to your new surroundings." I lived again through the past—the long past that had not returned to me in many years—all seemed fresh now as when I wandered over the bright scenes in my youthful happiness. Can this be possible, I said, that I meet you again more beautiful than before—truly, this is real, this is heaven, more of heaven, more of joy than the one we pictured in our earthly life—for does it not give us all of our brightest our happiest realities here again, full fresh in the embodiment of life, to be forever blessed—forever progressing and elevating one another.

This bright spirit said, "Follow me." She turned into a gorgeous palace, where I beheld in an arched room constellated with gems of rarest beauty, an art-gallery of paintings of our noblest, our most illustrious men and women of earth life, many who we would not find in the galleries of earth paintings, but who were known by soul teaching to be worthy of a place in the soul world.

Wealth or position had not brought them here, but the true, living soul that worked itself out in humility, ignoring suffering for the truth they would not deny. Could you see the soul speaking through the expression of the eye, you would wonder that they had been neglected while in earth life. Truly here was fit study for inspiration, living, breathing life startling out from those angelic works.

After viewing these, we were ushered into another room or arched dome, whose sides were filled with works of art and scientific lore—the sages, the poets, the painters, sculptors, philosophers, heroes and martyrs of every age and clime, who had expressed through these volumes their thought, their investigations, their trials and experiences gained while inhabitants of this earthly sphere.

Wonderful was this great library, and truly did I stand in wonder and amazement at this to me incomprehensible grandeur of what I saw before me. Still we moved on to another circular dome, when to my astonished gaze opened a museum of every tiling created on our globe from its first formation to the present time or at that time, for that was during my first introduction to spirit spheres. These are spirit designs before the earth is moulded into form, for spirit conceives and impregnates earth with its conception of everything that was made, whether life, vegetable or mineral. Thus we beheld the models of spirit life. Wonderful indeed, are thy works, O God, Thou great Divine; should we not give thanks to Thee whom to know is to love unspeakable and full of glory. The guide, for such this bright angel was, told me that all inventions or designs were preconceived in spirit-life and impressed upon those minds most susceptible and best adapted to such controls given at the time the world most needs them or can appreciate them—thus supplying her wants as fast as she demands—showing an all-wise power creating wants and supplying them. What a thought! that souls that hunger after food find their supply in spirit communion, whether through mechanical labor, mental lore or inspirational wisdom.

We now moved on. She said that she would take me to the homes of some who had been earth's poets. We came to a lovely spot where clustered beautiful trees and flowers, with miniature lakes and mounds which gave such a life scene that I felt chained to the spot.

Here were the homes of Shelly, Pope and Dryden, sages and philosophers in their earth time and age, resting in this sphere to revel again in those luxurious scenes of song, in which they loved to linger. Volumes of poems lay around, whose language had startled the world, and volumes that should arouse it again through other pens.

Such I found this beautiful locality—a living breathing witness of continued life. While we were contemplating of these beautiful homes, I was impressed to look at a lovely lake where were many spirits congregated. Following my guide, we approached to where they were gathered—when, suddenly, a shout of heavenly music broke upon my senses and swelled within those vibrating emotions of grandeur and sublimity that seemed to carry me to all that bad ever passed on to higher and holier realms of bliss. These were those whom I had long loved in sympathy, mingling together with those whose homes I had just passed. They came to us and seemed to recognize me by a peculiar tie that binds spirit to spirit.

We were welcomed to this beautiful retreat, and many were the inquiries for their home associations.

After passing a pleasant time, we returned to the home of my guide, when bidding me adieu, we parted.

My mother again approached, saying, "My son, we will now take you back to earth, where you may recognize the great sphere in which you will be guided and directed by those who will show you your mission."

I was happy to be permitted to revisit my home where all was dear to me; where many a friend still dwelt in the form to whom I longed to make known my happiness in being able to return to earth in the happy consciousness of being able to impart good if not to make myself known.

How eager did I again revisit old scenes, and how fresh came back to me all my past, and how truly gratified to be permitted this great blessing.

How I longed to make myself known to the dear ones left on earth. I was told that the time would come when I would be able to make myself known, be recognized as one who would be a friend to those still living upon the earth, that my duties on earth were only a commencement of continual life. That now I was being prepared to help those who still linger in bondage, to awaken those who slept in unconsciousness of their true life; that, that liberty for which I was an instrument to gain, had only commenced, and the continuation was a full, a free light for all to see, that should be as free to all as the sun's rays, that no one could hide or destroy; that it might illuminate all; that there should be no more oppression, no more bondage for man, but a free, universal freedom for all, an elevated spiritual condition of mankind; that they must be lifted out of this fear and darkness, and the angel world must mingle their sympathies and draw by their influence the souls of men out of bondage into confidence and love with God and the angel world.

How truly has to me that prophecy been fulfilled, that one of angels ministering unto the wants of men. Could man to-day, with all the great inspiration of this era, realize the wonderful changes being wrought out through angel ministry, he would not so often despair for the future.

What to man often looks dark and obscure may be the greatest of blessings in disguise. We trust too much to our powers and knowledge of eternal things and yield not enough to our interior promptings. When man learns to listen to the teachings from within, he will enable those loved friends to come nearer and impress them with the truthfulness of life.

I know, by my own experience, that I was helped much in my earthly life. I felt it then, but now I know. I was not the only one; thousands before me knew that great fact, and silently heeded it, and were blest accordingly.

For many years the world has been taught to deny those teachings as superstitious, and believers were called dreamers or fanatics, and utterly discarded in the world by popular teachings. Mothers and grandmothers have been looked upon as imbecil and deranged, who spoke of seeing or believing in "ghosts" or dreams; and many an honest, true-hearted, loving being, has been called a witch in communication with the devil, because she could tell of the future. Oh what dreadful darkness and superstition reigned in the days of witchcraft; how many bright souls were condemned and cruelly murdered by infatuated and misled beings, whose bigoted education and fear of a devil caused them to commit. Oh ignorance! how terrible are the revolutions which must roll over you to work out the great problem of a true life, whose inner essence is the aroma of all progress.

The angel world has ever ministered to the wants of man through all time, and had not bigotry and persecution ruled the earth with such a fearful hand, we might now be in sweet communion with the world, without doubt or fear. But those who have held power have used it to their own aggrandizement, and to sustain it have compelled the masses to ignorance and servitude, transferring God into a tyrant rather than a father.

Even when Christ was sent to enlighten and harmonize the world, he could not be recognized by them because he came not as they liked but as meek and lowly. How are the meek and lowly appreciated to-day, are they exalted or acknowledged? No. Such a spirit can never grow into a true spiritual condition, and the world cease to recognize the eternal as the one great aim of life. How many sacrifice dear and loving friends for the sake of being popular amongst those whose soul's aim is to shine like a flash of lightning while the bolt strikes its votary to the heart.

The cold formal teachings of theology has done its work upon the hearts of men; it has hardened them to other's goodness, and uplifted those who had its instructions as something better than a brother who does not see as they do.

If they would take Christ's example and teachings for their guide, striving to do as He did, with the same simple faith doing good and persecuting none, they would not remain idle, waiting for him to cleanse them from their sins by the blood He shed upon the cross. All that fail to learn that lesson in earth life, will have to learn it in the spirit; will have to learn that they have a work to do, and that if not done in earth life must be done in spirit, as no one can escape his mission. All "must work out their own salvation" in earth life or in the life to come.

Such were Christ's words as were impressed upon him and such all find it on coming here. Those who do not live with and by the spirit in earth life must work through that darkness after coming to spirit life. There are many phases or spheres through which spirit has to grow to become an independent spirit of the spheres. Many linger around earth years, having so much of the earthly about them that it attracts to itself all that belongs to it. If the spirit has not grown to a condition to free itself from its material, it will cling around until grown into a more spiritual condition. Thousands have to come back and take possession of other persons to carry out their unprogressed condition, and the more material their medium is, the better can spirits of that class act through them. All should endeavor to class their mediums according to their development, and not allow those progressed to a more spiritual plane to mingle with those of the earlier development in a social relation of circles unless as teachers. It is the same law as in governing schools. No teacher, for a moment, would bring himself down to the capacity of a scholar in the intellectual scale, expecting that scholar to be as well educated as himself, after having passed through many grades of education. But he may love, respect and mingle with them to instruct, to elevate them to a condition of knowledge. But to try to render himself as uneducated, would place him out of his condition, making it very inharmonious for both. Thus you see the same law governs both. We commence at the primary and rise in the progressive scale of intelligence. Infants are beautiful as miniature men and women, but they are not men and women for want of experience and knowledge, gained by the progressive life. This beautiful law of development gives a new light of usefulness through time and throughout eternity.

All are one great family, working out principles of life and assisting one another in the great workshop of eternity, all being perfectly arranged in harmony and beauty.

ON GOVERNMENT

"Your complex system of government needs and will receive reconstruction or remodeling. When we emerged from the revolutionary struggle, and came to give the fruits of our hard earned victory some definite shape in the formation of a government for the new nation, we adopted the articles of confederation as the best we could then devise. It required but a short time to teach us that they were defective, and that prudence and wisdom dictated something different and better. The constitution was consequently fashioned and superseded the confederation, and there has never been any disagreement as to the superior wisdom of the constitutional form of government, at least, as an improvement on the original confederation form. When this had been accomplished we were fully persuaded that the reorganization of the government under the constitution was the apex of statesmanship and the acme of the science of governmental construction, and were consequently happy and content. But alas, for poor human foresight. It very soon became evident that the new arrangement was imperfect, if not absolutely defective, and twelve amendments to the new constitution were proposed by Congress and ratified by the states. After and as the result of the late unhappy conflict between discordant states, or, rather, rebellion of certain states by secession against the rightful authority and sovereignty of the federal government, several additional amendments became necessary and imperative, and they were accordingly incorporated and ingrafted upon the already amended constitution. And now others are earnestly talked of and advocated; and does this not teach you the plain lesson that your system is still imperfect?

"The trouble is found to be that statesmanship is without foreknowledge, and is either blind to or oblivious of the requirements of the future. In other words, that the ceaseless mutations of human affairs, the ever acting and onward march of the law of change and progression, fail to strike the consciousness of statesmen or to secure their recognition. Of one thing you may be assured, your plan of government will be revised and remodeled to its vast betterment. When the time comes this will be most vehemently resisted by those who on all questions affecting the interests of the race and the happiness of mankind persist in remaining with the bats and owls of past ages rather than to be baptized in the light of the present and the foregleams of the future. But they must get out of the way of the car of progress or be crushed beneath its merciless and continually revolving wheels."

"FORGET YOUR POMPOUS PRIDE"

"Bring yourselves into a true union with God and his communing angels; and by the effort to reach the divine powers, your hearts will be filled with the upright living of a ceaseless beginning. Further, I may say, this generation is past the feelings of a united nation chosen by God for a holy purpose. Refer to him in the power of your earthly minds, and have regard for the Lord's kindness to you, and not pass it by with scorn. Lead poor dejected people by the hand of fellowship, and forget your pompous pride and high-toned dignity.

"George Washington is but a fly-speck to humanity's progress; and I must forget that I was ever more than a worm of the dust, sent by my Maker for some good purpose. I did not wholly go astray; but, O God! I was very nearly lost to heaven's door by so much VANITY. I no longer will inflict on you my own personalities. As a spirit, I have no memories that need renewing; but by your command I have retrospected a little, and for any good I am always ready."

Edgar Allan Poe, June 1849. (Public domain)

EDGAR ALLAN POE

As one of history's great writers of mystery and the macabre, it's no surprise that his ghost would be of interest to those who believed in communications with the dead. Plus, it was a fresh one. Poe died on October 7, 1849, about a year and a half after the Fox Sisters started the Spiritualism movement.

With Spiritualism being adopted by many religious figures eager to preach their values, Poe offered a voice that would attract many—and might cause some to reconsider their ways if he offered a new, more positive outlook on life and "truth" about death, such as in "The Dark World Described." And in some cases, he simply had more poetry to write. One medium, Lizzie Doten, claimed to have channeled Poe's spirit and recorded a collection of new works which she published in Poems from the Inner Life *in 1863.*

THE DARK WORLD DESCRIBED

EDGAR Poe, your friend by a call. What I am I never WAS. No, I am not in blindness, nor drunkenness, nor wickedness, nor mortal COIL. I now am a spirit given, through God's kind grace, to good works. For a thousand years, or eternities, as it seemed, I was with the blackest of spirit companions, as where else could I find rest or sympathy. Did I not seek this as my goal? Alas! too well I followed my desires and passions, led on, no doubt, by the passions of a devilish spirit, which the grace of God did not dispossess me of, and I did not ask. O false position! I did not understand my Creator's humble mercy toward his children. No kind spirit offered to write through my hand. But I think, many a dark spirit had my brain in his power—yea, the power of the demons of HELL. Blest and feeling friends, I will anticipate your wants, and offer you my experience in my life from sin.

My dear friends, I am Edgar Poe. Do you not remember the man who wrote the Tales of Woe? Too well I feel that I was groping for a good life, but the dangers that beset me thwarted any promptings that came for good; and when death announced that my life of follies was done, God! I shall never forget the heart-felt remorse that stopped or choked my spirit out of its happiness. On earth I was a drunken and benighted sot—lost to many loves, lost to much good, given to many temptations, and feeling no insight into my future victory or destruction. Alas! I now can vividly depict my first entrance into eternal life! It brings me right upon a thousand ills that have caused me the stings of a myriad of horrors. One does not realize the enormity of his crime when the tide is upon him, nor when the crime is present, for the moment; nor when he makes his life a fortress of crime. But when the light of day has past away forever, then does he seek relief when there is no one near to hear. My God! I felt as in a desert of black despair—or among a set of ravenous wolves, ready to devour me with hate, or laugh me down to perdition. My God! did I deserve such a meeting? Alas! I can but say that God is just, and I am what I made myself, except that he never forsook me in all my wickedness, nor pointed me to my hateful life. His spirit—it was that has lifted me up, up, up. My heavenly Father has shown me his tender mercies, and I have reached a goal of bliss that I never deserved; but in the Book of

Life it is written that it is the wandering sheep that needs the shepherd; and so with more care, through all my trials and wretchedness, he has found me, and led me with great patience to himself. And I will ask all weak and erring people of God's creation to give up RUM, to chase away the devil, to flee all temptations, and to follow God. Then you will never reap the sorrows of the wild and weak.

— EDGAR POE

THE LOST SOUL

Hark the bell! the funeral bell,
Calling the soul
To its goal.
Oh! the haunted human heart,
From its idol doomed to part!
Yet a twofold being bearing,
She and I apart are tearing;
She to heaven I to hell!
Going, going! Hark the bell!
Far in hell,
Tolling, tolling.
Fiends are rolling,
Whitened bones, and coffins reeking,
Fearful darkness grimly creeping
On my soul,
My vision searing,
She disappearing,
Drawn from me
By a soul I cannot see,
Whom I know can never love her.
Oh! that soul could I discover,
I would go,
Steeped in woe,
Down to darkness, down to hell!
Hark the bell! Farewell! farewell!

AN UNTITLED POEM

Written through the hand of medium Lizzie Doten.

From the throne of life eternal,
From the home of love supernal,
   Where the angels make music o'er the starry
      floor,
Mortals, I have come to meet you,
And with words of peace to greet you,
   And to tell you of the glory that is mine
      forevermore.

Once before. I found a mortal
Waiting at the heavenly portal—
   Waiting out to catch some echo from that
      ever-opening door;
Then I seized this quickened being,
And through all his inward seeing,
   Caused my burning inspiration in a fiery
      flood to pour.

Now I come more meekly human,
And the weak lips of a woman.
   Touched with fire from off the altar, not
      with burning, as of yore,
But in holy love descending.
With her chastened being blending,
   I will fill your soul with music from the
      bright celestial shore.

As one heart yearns for another,
As a child turns to its mother,
   From the golden gates of glory, turn I to
      the earth once more;
Where I drained the cup of sadness,
Where my soul was stung to madness,
   And life's bitter, burning billows swept my
      burdened being o'er.

Here the harpies and the ravens,
Human vampires, sordid cravens,
   Preyed upon my soul and substance, till I
      writhed in anger sore;
Life and I then seemed mismated.
For I felt accursed and fated,
   Like a restless, wrathful spirit, wandering
      the Stygian shore.

Tortured by a nameless yearning.
Like a fire-frost, freezing, burning,
   Did the purple, pulsing life-tide through its
      feeble channels pour;
Till the golden bowl, life's token,
Into shining shards was broken,
   And my chained and chafing spirit let from
      out its prison door.

But, whilst living, stirring, dying,
Never did my spirit cease crying:
   "Ye who guide the fates and furies, give, oh!
      give me, I implore—
From the myriad host of nations,
From the countless constellations,
   One pure spirit that can love me—one that
      I, too, can adore."

Through this fervent aspiration
Found my fainting soul salvation;
   Far from out its blackened fire quick did
      my spirit soar.
And my beautiful ideal,
Not too saintly to be real.
   Burst more brightly on my vision than the
      fancy formed Lenore.

'Mid the surging sea she found me,
With the billows breaking round me.

And my saddened, sinking spirit in her
    arms of love upbore;
Like a lone one, weak and weary,
Wandering in the mid-night dreary,
  On her sinless, saintly bosom, brought me
    to the heavenly shore.

Like the breath of blossoms blending,
Like the prayers of saints ascending,
  Like the rainbow's seven-hued glory, blend
    on souls forevermore;
Earthly lust and lore enslaved me,
But divinest love hath saved me,
  And I know now, first and only, how to live
    and how to adore.

O, my mortal friends and brothers!
We are each and all another's,
  And the soul which gives most freely from
    its treasures hath the more.
Would you lose life, you must find it,
And in giving love you bind it,
  Like an amulet of safety to your heart for-
    evermore.

SPIRIT POEM ON THE RAVEN

In 1856, Spiritualist reverend Thomas Lake Harris claimed to have channeled the spirit of Edgar Allan Poe, who apparently wanted to offer a new version of one of his most famous poems, The Raven. *Harris had just recently "discovered" his psychic powers, along with an ability to write poetry. He was known, in fact, to improvise his poetry rather quickly, which gave the impression that perhaps the words flowed from some otherworldly source. In this case, Poe. But before Poe's ghost rattled off a new* Raven, *he offered a brief introduction, explaining himself.*

My design, in this production, has been to embody, in Poetic drapery, the secret of my life. Being from my cradle a haunted man, conscious of more than human presence, and unable, from physiological and mental perversions, to analyze its essence, I grew morbid and melancholy.

This influence was that of my good guardian. Supernal visions, elevating and inspiring, descended from him to me. These visions became distorted in their descent. I wrote under Spiritual inspiration. My mediatorial condition was imperfect. I misapprehended and misinterpreted the Spiritual truth; hence the gloomy, misanthropic character of my productions.

I left the body to recover sanity; and then, in that mysterious, etherial, ideal world, discovered the pain-producing, vision-creating influence, operative in me in my earth-life, to have been, not demoniacal, but celestial.

Pity the man of genius. Madness itself, when accompanied with any degree of physical comfort, is Eden in comparison to the growth-pains of a mind, living in the unconscious violation of the Spirit's Law; forced to the rack of mental exertion to purchase bread; unable to compete with men of the world; crushed by unfeeling avarice; inly, vainly striving through all despair to give birth to deathless inspirations.—I have but partially expressed myself.

—E. A. P.

Fires within my brain were burning;
Scorning life, despairing, yearning,
Hopeless, blinded in my anguish, through
    my body's open door,
Came a Raven, foul and sable,
Like those evil birds of fable,
Downward swooping, where the drooping
    spectres haunt the Stygian shore.
—Not a bird, but something more.

Ghosts of agonies departed,
Festering wounds that long had
    smarted,
Broken vows, returnless mornings, griefs
    and miseries of yore,
By some art revived.—Undaunted
I gazed steadfast.—The enchanted,
Black, infernal Raven uttered a wild
    dirge-note evermore.—
Not a bird, but something more.

Gazing steady, gazing madly
On the bird, I spake, and sadly
Broken down too deep for scorning,
    sought for mercy to implore.
Turning to the bird I blessed it;
In my bosom I caressed it; .
Still it pierced my heart and revelled in
    the palpitating gore;—
'Twas a bird, and something more.

I grew mad. The crowding fancies
Black weeds they, not blooming
    pansies—
Made me think the bird a Spirit."—
"Bird," I cried, "be bird no more.

Take a shape; be man; be devil;
  Be a snake;—rise from thy revel;
From thy banquet rise;—be human;
    I have seen thee oft before;
    Thou art bird and something more.

"Tapping, tapping, striking deeper,
  Rousing Pain, my body's keeper,
Thou hast oft erewhile. sought entrance
    at the heart's great palace door.
  Take thy shape, O gloomy demon,
  Fiend, or spirit most inhuman,
Strike me through, but first, unvailing,
    let me scan thee o'er and o'er:
    Thou art bird, but something
      more."

Still, with sable pinions flapping,
  The great Raven, tapping, tapping,
Struck into my breast his talons; vast
    his wings outspread, and o'er
  All my nature cast a pallor;
  But I strove with dying valor,
With the poniard of repulsion striking
    through the form it wore;
    Not a bird, but something more.

"O, thou huge, infernal Raven,
  Image that Hell's King hath graven,
Image growing more gigantic, nursed
    beyond the Stygian shore,
  Leave me, leave me, I beseech thee,
  I would not of wrong impeach thee,"
I cried madly.—Then earth opened with
    a brazen, earthquake roar—
    Twas a bird,—a Demon more.
  Downward, downward, circling, speeding,

Cries of anguish still unheeding,
Striking through me with his talons,—still
    that Raven shape he bore,
Unto Erebus we drifted;
His huge wings by thunders lifted.
Beat 'gainst drifts of white flame-lightning,
    sprinkled red with human gore.
'Twas a bird, a Demon more.

"I'm no bird—an Angel, Brother,
A Bright Spirit and none other;
I have waited, blissful, tended thee for
    thirty years and o'er;
In thy wild, illusive madness.
In thy blight, disease and sadness,
I have sounded, tapping, tapping, at thy
    Spirit's Eden door:—
Not a bird, an Angel more!—

"Shining down with light Elysian,
    Through the pearly gates of vision,
On thy tranced, soul-lighted fancy, when,
    across thy chamber floor
Fell the Spirit-moonlight, laden
With soft dews from trees in Aidenn
Shaken downward-still nepenthe, drunk
    by dreaming bards of yore;—
Not a bird, an Angel more.

"In my Palmyrenian splendor,
    In Zenobian regnance tender,
More than Roman, though Aurelian were
    the kingly name I bore,
I have left my angel-palace,
    Dropping in thy sorrow's chalice
Consolation. O, 'twas blessed, sweet,
    thy pillow to bend o'er;—
Not a bird, an Angel more.

"Ended is life's mocking fever;

>   Where, through citron groves, for ever
> Blows the spice-wind and the love-birds
>   tell their rapture o'er and o'er,
>   From earth's hell by afrits haunted,
>   From its evil, disenchanted,
> I have borne thee; gaze upon me; didst
>   thou see me e'er before?—
>   Not a fiend, an Angel more."

William Shakespeare, copper engraving portrait by Martin Droeshout (1622). (Public domain)

WILLIAM SHAKESPEARE

The year 1916 marked the three hundredth anniversary of Shakespeare's death. Of course, a little thing like death could hardly slow the bard's pen. Over the years, the always-prolific writer continued to produce new works through the hands of mediums. At least, according to the mediums.

To celebrate his big tricentennial milestone, Shakespeare's spirit wrote Hamlet in Heaven *via automatic writing through the mediumship of Lincoln Phifer. Phifer claimed to have been receiving messages "purportedly" from Shakespeare for twenty years. When this* Hamlet *sequel was channeled in late 1915, Phifer claimed that "it did not enter my head at the time that 1916 was the third centennial of the death of Shakespeare, and the play, discussing death, seemed to be Shakespeare's contribution to the forthcoming world celebration of the event." Though the spirit never claimed his new play was intended to mark the commemoration, Phifer said he was "more than ever impressed with the feeling that he appreciated the honor that were being shown him on earth, when on the 14th of April, 1916, the anniversary of both his birth and death, he (or the influence signing itself Shakespeare) wrote the following two sonnets through my hand." They are as follows:*

> You say I died three centuries ago;
> You render homage to the words I uttered.
> If I were as I was I would bend low,
> And leave my Heaven for earth, being greatly flattered.
> But he who then was I is almost gone
> From my own memory as from human knowledge,
> And I that am feel that the blossoms thrown
> Do not reach me in this celestial college,
> I live so much that all life is my own;

I live so little that my past is dead;
But in your festivals I do take on
My olden life as you say what I said;
And as you cause me to know earth anew,
I owe my life and all its work to you.

Nature may die, but every year revives,
And she is always young and full of joy;
For dead fruits of old years she never grieves
But ever has the raillery of the boy.
The world is chewing old grains; it should stir
And free its infinite urge to life and zest,
Becoming young like phoenixes that were,
From ashes of the past in freshness dressed.
Why should the world moon over ancient words,
When spoken works of joy surpass them all?
Why should it seek to waken olden chords,
When Heaven and earth vibrate in carnival,
And when the sweetness of the thing that is
Sounds from the dead wood living minstrelcies?

As for Hamlet in Heaven, *Act 1 of this five-act play is reproduced here. In it, the ghost of Hamlet finds his father, who appeared as a ghost in the original* Hamlet.

Hamlet in Heaven

A Five Act Play

Purporting to Have Been Written

By William Shakespeare

By Automatic Writing
Through the Hand of

Lincoln Phifer

1916.
Published by Lincoln Phifer, Girard, Kansas
Price, 50c; 3 Copies, $1.00

HAMLET IN HEAVEN

Act One

Scene 1.—Hospital in abode of spirits. Hamlet discovered on a couch, with Nurse and Physician attending.

Physician—He wakens from his sleep.
Be ready with the nectar.
    (Hamlet stirs, opens his eyes and raises on his elbow.)

Hamlet—Where is Horatio?
Is he not here? Oh, if he goes to make
Report to clear my name, my blessings on him.
I see thy physic hath restored my life.
I thank thee not if still the king survives.
Or is Fortinbras the king?

  Phys.—He is the king.

  Ham.—Let my succession go to pithicoats;
I give my voice again for Fortinbras,
Glad if th' incestuous pig no longer
Reign over Denmark; for my head is twisted
And would not fit the crown. Tell me—my mother?

  Phys.—Hamlet, I have a story to unfold,
If thou art strong and brave enough to hear it.

  Ham.—After that I bore so many years
I'm strong enough to take the pack of Atlas;
And he who had the hardihood to open
The sluices to let out the royal life
Is brave enough to die, if need demand it.

  Phys.—But art thou brave enough to learn the truth,
That thou art dead?

  Ham.—Dead? I am not dead.

Phys.—Yet thy disgusted soul hath exit made
From gates of flesh.

Ham.—Give me my sword.
If I can swing it as I one time did,
I am not dead; if I can push its point
Into thy thigh, I live; if I can sheathe—.
But give me not the venomed instrument.

Phys.—It is not needful that thou take a sword.
Strike at me—so.
    (He squares his breast. Hamlet strikes at him, and his
    arm goes through physician's body.)

Ham.—Merciful Heavens!
Am I indeed among the shades of souls?
I flout the thought. Did I not see my father,
A spirit, when my belly bulged with woodcock?
Because I sense another, then, proves nothing.

Phys.—Hamlet is dead indeed.

Ham. (arising)—Then see how lively
A noble who hath passed his soul may be.
    (He dances; soon he soars off into the air.)
Lord! I am falling up! or do I dream it?
Is Hamlet mad indeed?

Nurse.—Mad, and worse,
For I have reason to declare it so.

Ham.—Who art thou?

Nurse.—I do not know. The name
Identifies one only to her friends,
And there are new names given us in Heaven.
Then, who I was thou need'st not ask; I am
What now I am; yet I am what I was,
Though only as a shade, a memory:
As one may be in fancy characters
He reads about.

Ham.—Pardon my inquiry.
At least thou seemest truthful. I appeal
To thee to tell the truth, this far at least:
Have I passed through the gates, as I am told?

Nurse.—Thou hast let loose of flesh.

Ham.—Where is my body? May I not look on it? If it is mine
Surely I have a right to see it who so lately
Fully commanded it.

Nurse.—It is for him to say.
  (Indicating physician.)

Ham.—Why may I not revisit the old home
And go in at the doors I know so well?

Phys.—The doors are sealed with ice, as much to thee
As to the veriest stranger. But be patient,
A quality of mind thou sometime lackest,
And later thou mayest look upon the clay
That held thy soul. But now it may not be.

Ham.—I command it, I who am a prince?

Phys.—Thou are no prince here, save in princely deed,
And thy command counts less than petulent children
Calling for sweets. Be guided by our counsel,
And we will lead thee into ways of peace;
Run wild, thou'lt dash thyself to laceration.

Ham.—I will be guided by thee. Am I sane?

Phys.—Perhaps no man is fully sane; perhaps
But few, even in the spirit, have such poise
They spin in perfect order, like a top
Newly struck out, nor wobble as they move.
We hope thou wilt regain thy normal balance
Without delay.

Ham.—I will be thy pupil.
Set me my lessons. Do I find myself

In blissful regions of the blest, or doomed
To wade the fiery streams of hell?

    Phys.—That thou shalt learn.

    (Curtain and end of scene.)

Scene 2.—Procession to the cemetery. Body of Hamlet is borne past, with new king and train and many people following. Hamlet, physician and nurse view from above.

    Ham.—Is that my body there?

    Phys.—It was thy body. Tis a lump of flesh
To which the worms hold title, now thy soul
Hath been evicted by the constable
Termed Death. Wouldst thou behold the face?

    Ham.—I never did, why should I do so now?
Why should I with the eyes they cannot see
Look on the eyes through which they one time saw,
And yet that see me not? Zounds! I will look.
'Tis an experience.
      (Draws near and gazes on the body)
Here is the face I've washed ten thousand times, but I no more
Shall play the varlet to it. Here's the cheek
The razor dragged across, which now requires
No hone or strop or lather; with its hairy harvest
This cheek was irrigated for new crop
With tears of sorrow at the pull I had.
Here is the dainty moustache that I fondled,
And deemed to charm the maids with these set wisps.
The mole behind the ear—good leech, is it
Upon my spiritual body? No? Ah, well,
There are worse things than death. These purple lips
The dear Ophelia kissed; what dubious taste!
These fingers handled more than I will name.
Would I had use of them, that I might choke
The fellows who so bear me to the dump.
That knave ate garlic ere he came to carry

My corpse to the garlic breeder. What sorry sight
His stomach is, when one may see therein!
Men are not beautiful beneath the skin.

   Phys.—Wouldst thou look on the form that was thy mother?

   Ham.—Not I; yet now I may be sure
The monkey of the north will not defile her.
Good leech, I fain would gaze upon her spirit,
To note the texture and the color of it.

   Phys.—Some day thou shalt. Let us pursue the things.
Before our noses.

   Ham.—As doth the common hound.

   Phys.—There is the chrysalis thy uncle shed.

   Ham.—Appropriately, they mean to mix his shell
With filth. God! I wish the clods would fall
Into his eyes and grate there; on his tongue,
And morgify his taste!

   Phys.—A bad sentiment.

   Ham.—The subject's bad.

   Phys.—Observe that Fortinbras
Hath given thee the honor; then thy mother;
Then Laertes; the late king comes last.

   Ham.—I did this fellow, Fortinbras, a service
By clearing paths for him. The late king last,
The new king first; this is philosophy.

   Phys.—Perhaps Horatio will eulogize
Thee, as they heave thee to the worms; let's see.
     (Procession stops at grave and corpses are lowered to the ground.
     Nobles and soldiers stand about, with populace in the background. Horatio stands at the head of Hamlet's body.)

   Horatio.—I wish to speak a word of my poor friend
And schoolmate, Hamlet. You supposed his mind

Soured and addled. If it were, small wonder,
Considering the churning that it had.
He was a youth, who, had he lived, would added,
As did his father, luster to the crown.
His judgment to the last shined like a star
Through rift of gathering clouds, in that he gave
His voice for Fortinbras. Think not of souls
He may have hurried to their great assize,
For they were few, but rather think upon
Your own lives and your childrens, that he saved
With his last thoughtful word. I will not tell,
For Hamlet's sake, the causes that combined,
Like ants about him, chained upon the hill
Of Denmark, to sting his frame to death
With most delicious torture. Here they lie,
Helpless to make defence; so let them be.
Remember Hamlet, as I shall, a youth
Of glorious promise, and the rest forget.
Turn to the future, there lies life. Behind
Is memory, and its twin, forgetfulness.

  (The corpses are lowered into the grave. Physician turns to Hamlet.)

 Phys.—Come, let us go.

 Ham.—No; stay. I wish to know
How 'tis to lie in dirt. Here side by side,
The stormy voyage o'er, we'll lie together
And stink in peace. I will not rip the king,
And he'll not brew a poison for my ear.
God be with thee, mother. Farewell, Hamlet-parings.
You'll look more wholesome when you turn to grass.
I raise my spirit arms above my head,
And having grown old in experience
Of death and my own funeral, I also
Grow holy and pronounce the benediction
Upon my little meeting on the earth.
Now let us take a turn 'round Heaven. Come.

  (Curtain and end of scene.)

Scene 3. Cloudland. Hamlet and Physician, strolling.

Phys.—Thou'lt mark that now the forms of air are plain
Before thy spiritual eye, and do not flit,
First in, then out the retina's range of vision,
As 'twas when in the flesh thy soul wast pent.
Thou seest that shadow yonder?

Ham.—I am not blind.

Phys.—Thank God for that. Thousands have not learned
To see with the spirit, so must range these swirls
And swells but stumblingly. They may indeed
Catch the impression of high spiritual lights
That seem to flit like flames, so that they feel
Plunged in the fires here, next in the shadows,
Dwelling in smoke. Dost thou know that shade?

Ham.—There's something in the walk that is familiar,
But I see not its face.

Phys.—It hath no face, For physiognomy is grown in Heaven,
As one on earth develops beard or bust.
That is thy father.

Ham.—My father?

Phys.—Yes.

Ham.—Poor, scarred, weak soul!
How he was wronged!

Phys.—Yea, by himself.

Ham.—By my uncle, rather,
And by my mother.

Phys.—They could not wrong him,
Except as he permit it. Did thy uncle
Drive th' unshriven soul from its tenement?
That event waited sometime, naturally;
And had the shade been ready for the change,
It would have found a mansion in the skies

Prepared for it by its development.
Wronged was thy father through the hasty marriage
Of her who was his wife, and he who was
His brother in the flesh? The thought is based
On the belief that somehow she was his,
A property, a slave—a mental picture
Which shows a rawness on the spiritual side.
Nothing can harm a man save he himself.

    Ham.—The shade approaches, I shall question him.

    Phys.—Do.

    Ham.—Oh, thou dark, troubled soul, tell me thy name,
For I believe I knew thee in the flesh,
And here await the confirmation of it.

    Hamlet, pere.—On earth I was a king, who
        now sweep through
Fires and smoke, hapless but yet not burned.
Hamlet I was, of Denmark.

    Hamlet, son.—My father!

    Hamlet, pere.—By what right
Dost thou apply the epithet to me?
If on my soul lies wrong to mother done,
Forgive me, and so open up my eyes
That I may see thy form, although unable
To scan thy features.

    Hamlet, son.—Oh, my poor father!
I am the fruit legitimate of thine,
Thine heir and thy avenger.
Look upon me, And tell thy Hamlet that I served thee well
In sending to their doom th' usurping king,
Thy brother and thy murderer, and she
Who was thy wife and my unhappy mother.

    Hamlet, pere.—And art thou Hamlet? I can see but only
        A shadow where thou art. And is she dead

Who was my wife, thy mother? Tell me how
She perished.

Hamlet, son.—She drank the poison
The king, thy murderer, meant for my lips,
Not knowing it was poison.

Hamlet, pere—It is well.
She perished as I did, although the poison
Entered our body walls through differing channels.

Phys.—If I may say so, who am a physician,
It is thy passion, thy mean spirited
Desire for revenge, that keeps thy soul
Blind and in fires where there are no fires.
Let go such thoughts.

Hamlet, pere.—I am a king.
Thou sayest my brother died. Tell me the manner.

Hamlet, son.—I thought they in this world knew everything.

Phys.—How little know they who imagine so!

Hamlet, son.—I deemed thy eyes were on me when I did it;
For I, being beguiled to fence with Laertes,
Was pricked with weapon that, unknown to me,
Had deadly poison at the tip. Recovering,
And changing weapons, Laertes was pinged,
And in act of death revealed the plot;
On which I turned the point upon the king
And dragged him here with me; though I mistrust
He hath escaped me, for my eyes have not
Lighted upon him here.

Hamlet, pere.—If thou shouldst find him,
Hamlet, I charge thee, if thou findest him,
Bring me to him, and guide my fingers to
The throat of that betrayer.

Phys.—Thou art not a king,
But a mere groveler.

Hamlet, son.—What meanest thou?
Remember who it is to whom thou speakest,
And do not force me to compel respect
For betters than thou art; for rudeness tops
Gratitude for service.

    Phys.—I am thy elder
In this land where there is no royal blood
Because there is no blood. We equals stand,
And he alone is greatest who most knows,
Sees clearest, serves the most. In kindness spake I,
Wishing to cure the blindness of the sire,
And lead thee, Hamlet, patient given me,
To healthier thoughts. Feelings of enmity,
Revenge and pride, bedwarf the soul, or here
Or in the flesh. Cast such things from thee.
Walk humbling and inherit every good,
Walk proudly and be blind and fall to harm.
    (Hamlet, pere and son, appear astonished, outraged,
      and are silent.)
Well, is it will, or must?

    (Curtain and end of act.)

SONNETS
of
SHAKESPEARE'S GHOST

The Words procured by GREGORY THORNTON
The Ornaments made by WILLEM BLAEU

Never before Imprinted

AT SYDNEY
By *Angus & Robertson*, and are to be solde
by all booksellers
1920

SONNETS OF SHAKESPEARE'S GHOST

In 1920, Gregory Thornton "procured" a series of sonnets from Shakespeare's ghost. He compiled the works into a book that he simply titled, Sonnets of Shakespeare's Ghost. *Three sonnets and Thornton's brief introduction to the book follow.*

The Spirit of William Shakespeare, sore vexed of them who say that in his Sonnets he writ not from the truth of his heart but from the toyings of his brain, and that he devised but a feigned object to fit a feigned affection, herein maketh answer, renewing as best a shadow may that rhyme wherein he was more excellent in the living body.

I.
THE wise world saith I not unlock'd my heart
When I of thee and thy dear love did write,
And would each word of mine to false convert,
Doing my simple sense a double spite.
It saith thou wert but shadow born of nought,
But vain creation of an apish rhyme,
While, Fashion's fool, my strain'd invention sought
To better them who best did please the time.
But wherefore say they so, and do dear wrong
To thee, whose worth was my sole argument,
To me, whose verse 'twas truth alone made strong
By that the breast must feel, not brain invent?
    They who this doubt never such beauty knew,
    Nor what to poet love alone can do.

II.
THEY say a man ne'er bore such love to man,
Or, if he did, 'twere but a cause for shame;
But, speaking so, they their own measure scan,
And blot their censure with self-blaming blame.

For, thou being Beauty's best, the best of me
Worshipp'd but Beauty's self and Beauty's worth;
My fire and air, my spirit, adored thee
Unmix'd with gross compounding of my earth.
And thou wert best of Truth, the first in grace
Of all rich gems in Virtue's carcanet;
Then should I not love thee and give thee place
Above all love of sense on woman set?
    In love of Beauty, whate'er shape 'tis in,
    There's nought of Truth, if it must think of sin.

III.
LOOK, when the rose to deep vermilion hue
Adds that sweet odour gracious Nature gives,
When his proud glory gladdens every view,
And no base worm within his beauties lives,
We nothing question of what sex it be,
Nor ask more of it than that it should lend
His lovely gaze for ravish'd eye to see,
And on the blessed air his fragrance spend.
We ask not that the star which lights the heaven
Should be or male or female to our sense,
Suffic'd in this, that it empearls the even,
And happies all our under reverence.
    Then might'st not thou, who wert both rose
        and star,
    Be pure to me as these to others are?

AN INTERVIEW

Readers may have enjoyed Shakespeare's new works, whether they believed they were written by his ghost, impostor ghosts, or just very clever mediums. But if they wanted to hear about Shakespeare's own experiences and feelings beyond the veil, they could turn to Henry Kiddle's 1879 book, Spiritual Communications. *Kiddle assures his readers that "not a single communication has been inserted which was not written through the mediumship of the editor's daughter or son" and that he was present for most of these communications. Therefore, he "knows they are not the offspring of imposture or delusion. They come from the 'world of spirits.'"*

Q.—Have you any regrets for your writings while on earth?
A.—Yes, sorrowful to mention. What a lost sheep I was from my Shepherd's light! Would to God Almighty I had felt his strength of understanding the world and its inhabitants! I did well. Perhaps, I did not lose all my talents; but most were thrown away, or, what is worse, led astray many from God's works. Certainly, my teachings through the drama were not bad, but not altogether elevating to the minds of the weak in spiritual lore.

Q.—What is your present opinion of your play of Hamlet?
A. It is too sentimental.

Q.—In what respect?
A.—I think it should have been on a purer motive.

Q.—What do you think of Macbeth?
A.—Better in its moral teachings.

Q.—Did you not introduce much of the spiritual in it?
A.—Yes, by inspiration.

Q.—What do you mean by that?
A.—Mode of taking my inspirational ideas.

Q.—Which do you consider the purest of your plays? (*The Medium wrote obscurely, apparently not being able to take the impression of the name. The*

editor manifesting some impatience to obtain a response, it was written : —)
A.—Oh! you must not seek too much through the medium.

Q.—Of course, you know your works still give great pleasure to mankind?
A.—Yes, to my humble regrets. They might and should have been nearly perfect in their holy teachings to my people, who patiently endured their weak oncomings; but, praised be God, I did the best in the power of my understanding, and was not too vain to see that I was but a weak instrument in the hands of the Potter.

Q.—If we should publish these revelations, what would you desire we should say as coming from you?
A.—Say that I am the teacher of the people's pleasure, in preparing their hearts to see that the drama of life is but a side play to the eternal teachings that are found in one word of God's book, or in one look from your Saviour's divine eyes to throw the blessing of his divine love upon your souls. Do you not see that my teachings were somewhat selfish, because I took from God his right of providing a home for the soul? But, notwithstanding this bare-faced contradiction to the statement of his Word, I have found favor and grace in his supreme sight, and am nevertheless happy!!!

Q.—What do you mean by "taking from God his right of providing a home for the soul"?
A.—I mean that I did not use the means of throwing God's passion to the light, instead of this world's affairs entirely.

Q.—But did you not introduce much of the spiritual element in your plays?
A.—Yes, but not so strong as I should. It was merely visionary.

Q.—How about the spirit of Hamlet's father?
A.—He was a stupid scapegoat.

Q.—Scapegoat for whom?
A.—For the spirits of the heavenly creating.

Q.—Will you write a brief poem descriptive of your heavenly joy?

(The following was written:—)

"My joy in heaven
Is from the seven
Of the truths of God's creating:
First comes the queen
Of love; then she
Who blesses the pure in heart,—your
Everlasting friend,
Benevolence.

"Second, comes the God-
Dess of supreme
Delight, called Satisfaction,
To teach you that
All things are for
Your heart's benefaction.

"Then, third, the Light
From heavenly thoughts,
To bless your soul's identity;
So on, to the seven,
As shown in the old
Fables of heathen idolatry."

Portrait of Mark Twain by A.F. Bradley, 1907.

MARK TWAIN

Mark Twain was not a Spiritualist, though he was known to attend séances purely for the entertainment value. The beloved American writer and humorist died in 1910, but wasn't done writing. A medium and novelist named Emily Grant Hutchings, working with another medium, Lola V. Hays, claimed Twain spelled out two short stories and a novel, one letter at a time through a Ouija board between 1915 and 1917: Up the Furrow to Fortune, A Daughter of Mars, and Jap Herron.

"That the story of Jap Herron and the two short stories which preceded it are the actual post-mortem work of Samuel L. Clemens, known to the world as Mark Twain, we do not for one moment doubt," Hutchings wrote in her introduction to the novel. "His individuality has been revealed to us in ways which could leave no question in our minds."

Critics were not fond of Twain's posthumous novel. The New York Times wrote, "If this is the best that 'Mark Twain' can do by reaching across the barrier, the army of admirers that his works have won for him will all hope that he will hereafter respect that boundary."

Chapters One and Two of this posthumous work are included here. But first, indulge yourself in an interview Twain granted to another medium in 1919 for Azoth, an occult magazine.

Today, Twain's name remains connected to the spirit world. His Hartford, Connecticut, house is believed to be haunted, particularly by his daughter, Susy, who died in 1896 of spinal meningitis in the house while Twain was in Europe.

A CHAT WITH MARK TWAIN
By A Psychic Scribe

SINCE Mark Twain left this world and departed to the land of spirits he has made several attempts to prove that he is still living and is able to communicate with those on earth. A number of messages, alleged to have been received from him, have been given to the world through mediums of repute, and some of these messages have all the characteristics of the famous writer who once amused the reading public.

Always full of sprightly wit, and delivering his wisdom in an atmosphere of humor, Mark Twain seems to have carried this mannerism into the world beyond. The messages that he has delivered are full of wit and quaint philosophy. His capacity for work, moreover, seems to have remained undiminished, for already two books, received by means of the Ouija board, have been published by an enterprising medium who succeeded in getting into close touch with him, and was able to record his brilliant utterances.

As the result of a recent psychic experience, I have been enabled to add another Mark Twain message to those which have already appeared. The means by which I obtained this communication were similar to those employed by other mediums; that is to say, I had a lead to the subject, and a link with the spirit plane was apparently formed in response to my desire for information.

I had been reading Dr. Hyslop's new book, "Contact With the Other World," in which the author has devoted a great deal of space to the Mark Twain messages, received through mediums, and has expressed a firm belief in the authenticity of "Jap Herron," one of the posthumous books that Mark Twain is said to have dictated.

After I had read Dr. Hyslop's work, I felt a strong desire to get into communication with Mark Twain, for the purpose of getting his opinion of the book and interviewing him on other topics of interest. I have devoted much time to automatic writing in recent years, and from previous experiences I had an intuition that conditions for communicating were satisfactory. Taking up my pad and pencil, I made an effort to be receptive and in a few minutes a message came through.

Before quoting the conversation that followed, I must state that some weeks before I had received what purported to be a message from Mark Twain, which failed to keep to the point and was so rambling that at last I wrote, rather petulantly, "If you are Mark Twain, please try to dictate like a literary genius and not like a mountebank."

When I started my conversation after reading Dr. Hyslop's book, I had completely forgotten the "mountebank" incident. Mark Twain, however, had apparently remembered it, and the occurrence evidently rankled in his spirit mind.

This will explain his ironical references to the term "mountebank" which appear in my talk with him. After communication had been established I received a remark about the book, which was followed by my questions and the spirit answers. The record is as follows:

M. T.— Well, all has been settled by the learned man who wrote the book which you have just been reading. He did not lead the reader away into the realms of darkness and leave him there, but he wrote as a seer and prophet of the new dispensation.

Q. — If this is Mark Twain, can you give some proof of identity?
A.— All your attention, my friend, seems to be directed to the hearing part. Your mental sight isn't very strong or my identity would be realized at once.

Q.— I am careful because, in many cases, automatic writers are imposed upon by their own sub-conscious thinking, which directs the writing of messages.
A.— Hear, hear, most learned friend. You are a healthy and active personality, even if you are not a very sensitive medium at times.

Q. — A typical message from Mark Twain ought to be full of jokes and funny sayings.
A.— Beneath the pages of Mark Twain's books a lesson is to be read by all who have eyes—the setting free of the soul from restraint, and deliverance from the narrow ideas of social decorum which have strangled humanity. That was disguised beneath his quips and laughter which drew so much attention from the world.

Q. — It is asserted by some people that "Jap Herron" is only a weak imitation of your writing style. What have you to say about that?
A. — World desires are never satisfied, because we invariably see that all is vanity and vexation of spirit, but over here the material side has no hold on the spirit, while the mental side is realized in all its greatness and perfection.

Q. — You are not speaking to the point. Your reply is rather incoherent.
A. — The answer may seem rambling, but, my dear friend, be a little patient with a hardened old writer who was once on earth as a maker of books and has temporarily deserted the spirit world to reason with you about life. You referred to me lately as a mountebank, but mountebanks are sometimes a little more learned than some philosophers who are decently trained in life's niceties.

Q. — You seem to suggest that I applied the term "mountebank" to you. I have no recollection of ever having done so.
A. — You deleted the word from your memory, but the sting remained in mine, and was only removed when you desired to treat me with some degree of respect. Never mind, here is my spirit hand to shake and be friendly.

Q. — Peace having been restored, I would like to ask you a question. Why is it that I occasionally lose the art of automatic writing and fail to get any communications from beyond?
A. — You destroy the faculty at times because you suspect that it is some mountebank performance of your own mind, or of some tricky influence that is masquerading as a spirit. You deny in your own heart that the messages are bona fide, and thus destroy your receptive power.

> (This statement, I may add, is true. Although I am a believer in the possibility of spirit communication, my faith is shaken sometimes when I receive misleading messages or read an adverse opinion regarding survival, expressed by some man of science.)

Q. — What do you think of the present state of the world?
A. — From what I can learn, I must confess that I am very glad not to be in the world at the present time, because it seems that the relative

positions of souls are such that the great are mostly on the lower tier, while the less desirable invariably manage to get on top of the pile. As things are, men are retarding their ascent to a higher realm by their mental working, which is so deadly in its material outlook that only a cataclysm could ever awaken them to anything else. Money and power are still the great prizes for which all humanity seems to be struggling, and when the struggle is over how poor even the wealthiest appear on this side of the river.

Q.— Why don't you say something about the spirit world instead of repeating things that most of us know already?
A.— My learned friend says "Why not tell us all about the spirit world," and he is also mentally adding, "set our minds at rest about whether there is a heaven or a hell." Now, here is my reply: Some are over here who were doomed to hell, but they are happy and are seeing heaven as their reward. Others, who were made to believe that they would surely wear golden crowns, are what a really candid man would term seeing a hell of a lot more than they ever expected. In other words, they are reaping a full harvest of selfish desires and aspirations, while the relentless hand of justice awards bliss to those who were not saintly outside, but were devout in their souls and saintly in their hearts and actions.

Q.— I wish you would say what could be done to prove the existence of the spirit world beyond all doubt, so that skepticism would be ended.
A.— Men are getting a few glimpses of the spirit world by means of a few headstrong souls who insist upon returning to earth to announce that they are still alive; some are hearing of the life beyond through their own intuitions, and some are getting help in other ways. But none are ever so thoroughly convinced that they are able to say with positive assurance, "I know that life is continued on another plane, and all my doubts have ended." There is still a lingering suspicion that they may have been deceived by the evidence.

The only way to set at rest all these doubts is by having a real sense of life beyond, which is only possible by so leaving the material life as to be able to view the spiritual as a reality. And that is only possible by setting free the soul and directing its flight to the next world. To accomplish that is only possible when the sentient desires are so developed that lead is given to the aspirant. No sort of proof will ever be given that will convince all men until they become more thoroughly developed in their spiritual attributes and less governed by material desires.

Q.— How about the materialized spirits that appear at seances? They are very good proof, and so are the communications received through genuine mediums.
A.— What you really desire is, for a spirit to appear and deliver a message to incredulous scientists and other skeptics, but no such deliverance is possible, because the sentient matter which develops at seances is dependent upon the medium, and is not capable of wandering about, all over the earth, setting hard, callous humanity at rights on the subject of spiritualism. Mediums are not able to set up a permanent connection with the spirit world, and the shapes they develop by their faculty of reproduction are rather the reflection of the soul than its actual embodiment.

Q.—Then there is no way in which we can get satisfactory proof without trance conditions or other abnormal states?
A.— No; because the hold of the material is far too strong to enable the spirit world to become visible to mortal life in the ordinary sense.

Q.— One of our scientific friends is going to start a psychical laboratory and catch ghosts. That will probably furnish the world with some startling evidence.
A.— He has a meritorious object, but he has a hopeless task before him, because no one on earth will ever succeed in catching a spirit with scales, test tubes and sound registers.

Q.—It is so hard to prove the existence of spirit life that it is not surprising many of us feel our faith weakening at times.
A.— If you would retain your power to communicate you must write as a believer and not as a disbeliever in the higher powers of the unseen world. My dear friend, you must learn that the mind is stronger than the mouldy life of earth, and that intelligent mankind is not as the beasts that perish in their ignorance of the truth.

Q.— Can you dictate a message to the readers of Azoth?

TO AZOTH THINKERS

A.— Yes, take this down, and give it to the editor: "Mountebanks are honest, even if they are standing on their heads at times instead of on their feet as learned writers are always accustomed to stand. When the sentiment is honest, however, and the heart is sound, what difference does it make where the mountebank stands or how he stands? Spirits are not as the solid, dignified citizens who are seldom caught in a position that is not strictly in accordance with the rules of earthly etiquette. Where all is more or less misty, our notions of etiquette must, of course, be a trifle hazy.

"Well, it is satisfactory to learn that Azoth has joined the ranks of the publications that are telling the truth to a very unappreciative world. Those who have been associated with the editor have done good work toward finding the solution of life's greatest problem-the destiny of mankind after earthly existence is ended.

"Let me tell you this: the material is not strong enough to hold the spirit, and nothing can ever destroy the soul. Here is a living proof of the truth—myself—a most determined opponent of all that is false. I hope that Azoth will work on and mould the thoughts of at least a few people to understand the whole truth and nothing but the truth. "Beneath the heart of honesty lies the soul of truth, and on that reason enthrones herself as supreme judge. No reversal of her decisions is ever necessary. When men are governed by her rulings the world will be a more decent place of residence for all who believe in good, hard common sense and freedom of soul.

"Even the strongest arguments are useless to convince the world that life after death has been proved by experience. All that most progressive editors are able to do is to relate such happenings as are reported by the Society for Psychical Research and leave the rest to reason.

"'Willie, we have missed you,' says the good old song, but the sentiment is only half true, for if the song were as real as life it would add, 'For heaven's sake don't come back, or you'll scare us into a fit.' Such is the attitude of the clergy and other earthbound folk. They are against all return of the spirit, because it is a reflection on their favorite doctrines of heaven and hell and bodily resurrection. But here is a mountebank, all alert in returning to deny their stories of the future life.

"It is no good to write to the half-witted people who are homeward bound, and yet refuse to have the home revealed before they arrive there. Azoth is leading some to think, but the great majority of people in the world are as material as a row of bricks in a wall, and are just about as capable of original thinking.

"Well, I am glad to be able to send my greetings, and to show the editor that I am not vindictive in the slightest degree, in spite of all that has been said about me in *Azoth*. Would that I could say something more readable, and relate some experiences worth repeating. But, here, I am tired of standing on my head, and really I must get on my feet before the celestial police request me to move on."

— MARK TWAIN

JAP HERRON
CHAPTER I

As every well-bred story has a hero, and as there seems better material in Jap than any other party to this story, we will dignify him. Mary Herron feebly asserted her rights in the children by naming them respectively, Fanny Maud, Jasper James and Agnesia. Jasper deteriorated. He became Jap, and Jap he remained, despite the fact that Fanny Maud developed into Fannye Maude and Agnesia changed her cognomen, without recourse to law, to Mabelle. The folks in Happy Hollow continued to say "Magnesia" long after she left its fragrant depths.

The father of the little Herrons was a kingfisher. He spent his hours of toil on the river bank and his hours of ease in Mike's place. One Friday, good luck peered through the dingy windows of the little shanty where the Herrons starved, froze or sweltered. It was Friday, as I remarked before. Mary was washing, against difficulties. It had rained for a week. The clothes had to dry before Mary could cash her labor, and it fretted Jacky Herron sorely. His credit had lost caste with Mike, and Mike had the grip on the town. He had the only thirst parlor in Happy Hollow. So Jacky smashed the only remaining window, broke the family cup, and set forth defiantly in the rain. And in the fog and slashing rain he lost his footing, and fell into the river. As it was Friday, Mary had hopefully declared that luck would change—and it did!

The town buried Jacky and moved his family into decent lodgings, because the Town Fathers did not want to contract typhoid in ministering to them. Loosed of the incubus of a father, the little family grew in grace. Jappie, as his baby sister called him, was the problem. Agnesia was pretty, and the Mayor's wife adopted her. Fanny Maud went west to live with her aunt, and Jap remained with his mother until she, after the manner of womankind, who never know when they have had luck, married another bum and began supporting him. Jap ran away.

He was twelve years old, red-headed, freckled and lanky, when he trailed into Bloomtown. He loafed along the main street until he reached the printing office, and there he stopped. An aphorism of his late lamented dad occurred to him.

"Ef I had a grain of gumption," said dad, during an enforced session of his family's society, "I would 'a' went to work in my daddy's printin' office, instid of runnin' away when I was ten year old. I might 'a' had money, aplenty, 'stid of bein' cumbered and helt down by you and these brats."

Jap straggled irregularly inside and heard the old Washington hand press groan and grunt its weary way through the weekly edition of the *Herald*. After the last damp sheet had been detached from the press, and the papers were being folded by the weary-eyed, inky demon who had manipulated the handle, he slouched forward.

"Say, Mister," he asked confidently, "do you do that every day?" indicating the press, "'cause I'm goin' to work for you."

The editor, pressman and janitor looked upon him in surprise and pity.

"I appreciate your ambition," he said, more in sorrow than anger, "but I have become so attuned to starving alone that I don't think I could adjust myself to the shock of breaking my fast on you."

Jap was unmoved.

"My dad once thought he'd be a editor, but he got married," he said calmly. "Sensible dad," commented the editor, with more truth than he dreamed. "I suppose that he had three meals a day, and a change of socks on Sunday."

"But Ma had to get 'em," argued Jap. "I want to be a editor, and I am agoin' to stay." And stay he did.

CHAPTER II

"Run out and get a box of sardines," ordered the boss of the Washington press. "I've got a nickel. I can't let you starve. I lived three months on them—look at me!"

Jap surveyed him apprehensively.

"I'd hate to be so thin," he complained, "and I don't like sardines nor any fishes. My dad fed us them every day. Allus wanted to taste doughnuts. Can I buy them?"

Ellis Hinton laughed shortly, and spun the nickel across the imposing stone. Jap caught it deftly. An hour later he appeared for work, smiling cheerfully.

"Why the shiner?" queried Ellis, indicating a badly swollen and rapidly discoloring eye.

"Kid called me red-top," said Jap bluntly.

"Love o' gracious," Ellis exclaimed, "what is the shade?"

"It's red," quoth Jap, "but it ain't his business. If I am agoin' to be a editor, nobody's goin' to get familiar with me."

This was Jap's philosophy, and in less than a week he had mixed with every youth of fighting age in town. The office took on metropolitan airs because of the rush of indignant parents who thronged its portals. Ellis pacified some of the mothers, outtalked part of the fathers and thrashed the remainder. After he had mussed the outer office with "Judge" Bowers, and tipped the case over with the final effort that threw him, Jap said, solemnly surveying the wreck:

"If I had a dad like you, I'd 'a' been the President some day."

Ellis gazed ruefully into the mess of pi, and kicked absently at the hell-box.

"I'll work all night," cried Jap eagerly. "I'll clean it up."

"We'll have plenty of time," said Ellis gloomily. "We have to hit the road, kid. Judge Bowers owns the place. He has promised to set us out before morning."

But luck came with Jap. It was Friday again, and Bowers's wife presented him with twins, his mother-in-law arrived, and his uncle inherited a farm. There was only one way for the news to be disseminated, and he came in with his truculent son and helped clean up, so that the *Herald* could be issued on time. More than that, he made the boys shake hands, and concluded to put Bill to work in the *Herald* office. After he had puffed noisily out, Ellis looked whimsically at Bill.

"Are you going to board yourself out of what I am able to pay you?" he asked.

"Oh, I don't reckon Pappy cares about that," the boy said cheerfully. "He just wants to keep me out of mischief, and he said that lookin' at you was enough to sober a sot."

Months dragged by. Bill and Jap worked more or less harmoniously. Once a day they fought; but it was fast becoming a mere function, kept up just for form. Ellis was doing better. He had set up housekeeping, since Jap came, in the back room of the little wooden structure that faced the Public Square, and housewives sent them real food once in a while.

Once Ellis feared that Jap was going to quit him for the Golden Shore. It was on the occasion of Myrtilla Botts's wedding, when she baked the cakes herself, for practice, and her mother thoughtfully sent most of them to the Editor, to insure a big puff for Myrtilla. Ellis was afraid; but Jap, with the enthusiasm and inexperience of youth, took a chance. Bill was laid up with mumps, or the danger would have been lessened. As it was, it took all the doctors in town to keep Jap alive until they could uncurl him and straighten out his appendix, which appeared to be cased in wedding cake. This experience gave Jap an added distaste for the state of matrimony.

"My dad allus said to keep away from marryin'," he moaned. "But how'd I know you'd ketch it from the eatin's?"

The subscription list grew apace. There was a load of section ties, two bushel of turnips and six pumpkins paid in November. Bill and Jap went hunting once a week, so the larder grew beyond sardines. Jap acquired a hatred of turnips and pumpkins that was in after years almost a mania. At Christmas, Kelly Jones brought in a barrel of sorghum, "to sweeten 'em," he guffawed. Jap had grown to manhood before he wholly forgave that pleasantry. It was a hard winter. Everybody said so, and when Jap gazed at Ellis across the turnips and sorghum of those weary months, he said he believed it.

"Shame on you," rebuked Ellis, gulping his turnips with haste. "Think of the wretched people who would be glad to get this food."

"Do you know any of their addresses?" asked Jap abruptly. "Because I can't imagine anybody happy on turnips and sorghum. I'd be willin' to trade my wretched for theirn."

Kelly said that Jap would be fat as butter if he ate plenty of molasses, and this helped at first; but when the grass came, he begged Ellis to cook it for a change.

When George Thomas came in, one blustery March day, to say that if the turnips were all gone, he would bring in some more, Ellis pied Judge Bowers's speech on the duties of the Village Fathers to the alleys, when he saw the malignant look that Jap cast upon the cheery farmer.

Once a week Bill and Jap drew straws to determine which one

should fare forth in quest of funds, and for the first time in his brief business career, Jap was glad the depressing task had fallen to him. "Pi" was likely to bring on an acute attack of mental indigestion, and the boy had learned to dread Ellis Hinton's infrequent but illuminating flame of wrath.

The catastrophe had been blotted out, the last stickful of type had been set and Bill had gone home to supper when Jap, leg-weary and discouraged, wandered into the office. Ellis looked up from the form he was adjusting.

"How did you ever pick out this town?" the boy complained, turning the result of his day's collection on the table.

Ellis turned from the bit of pine he was whittling, a makeshift depressingly familiar to the country editor. He scanned the meager assortment of coins with anxious eye. Jap's lower jaw dropped.

"I'll have to fire you if you haven't got enough to pay for the paper."

"Got enough for that," said Jap mournfully, "but not enough for meat."

"Didn't Loghman owe for his ad?" Ellis demanded. "Did you ask him for it?"

"Says you owe him more 'n he's willin' for you to owe," Jap ventured.

Ellis sighed.

"Meat's not healthy this damp weather," he suggested. "Cook something light."

"It'll be darned light," said Jap. "There's one tater."

"No bread?" asked Ellis.

"Give that scrap to the cat," Jap returned, "Doc Hall says she's done eat all the mice in town and if we don't feed her she'll be eatin' off'n the subscribers."

"Confound Doc Hall," stormed Ellis. "You take your orders from me. That bread, stewed with potato, would have made a dandy dish." He shook the form to settle it, and faced Jap.

"How did I come to pick this place?" he said slowly. "Well, Jap, it was the dirtiest deal a boy ever got. I had a little money after my father died. I wanted to invest it in a newspaper, somewhere in the West, where the world was honest and young. I had served my apprenticeship in a dingy, narrow little New England office, and I thought my lifework was cut out for me. I had big dreams, Jap. I saw myself a power in my town. With straw and mud I wanted to build a town of brick and stone. Dreams, dreams, Jap, dreams. Some day you may have them, too."

He let his lean form slowly down into a chair. Jap braced himself against the table as the narrative continued:

"In Hartford I met Hallam, the man who started the Bloomtown *Herald*. I heard his flattering version. I inspected his subscription list and studied the columns of his paper, full of ads. I bought. The subs were deadheads, the ads—gratuitous, for my undoing. It was indeed straw and mud, and, lad, it has remained straw and mud." He leaned his head on his hand for a moment.

"That was the year after you were born, Jap. I was only twenty-one. For a year I was hopeful; then I dragged like a dead dog. You will be surprised when I tell you what brought me to life again. I tell you this, boy, so that you will never despise Opportunity, though she may wear blue calico, as mine did.

"It was one dark, cold day. No human face had come inside the office for a week. That was the period of my life when I learned how human a cat can be. We were starving, the cat and me, with the advantage in favor of the cat. She could eat vermin. I sat by the table, wondering the quickest way to get out of it. Yes, Jap, the first and, God help me, the only time that life was worthless. The door opened and a plump woman dressed in blue calico, a sunbonnet pushed back from her smiling face, entered."

To Jap, who listened with his heart in his throat, it seemed that Ellis was quoting perhaps a page from the memoirs he had written for the benefit of his townsmen. His deep, melodious voice fell into the rhythmic cadence of a reader, as he continued:

"'Howdy, Mr. Editor,' she chirped. 'I've been keenin' for a long time to come in to see you. I think you are aprintin' the finest paper I ever seen. I brought you a mess of sassage and a passel of bones from the killin'. It's so cold, they'll keep a spell. And here's a dollar for next year's paper. I don't want to miss a number. I am areadin' it over and over. Seems like you are agoin' to make a real town out of Bloomtown,' and with a friendly pat on the arm, she was gone."

Ellis brushed the long hair from his brow, the strange modulation went out of his voice and the fire returned to his brown eyes as he said:

"Jap, I got up from that table and fell on my knees, and right there I determined that starvation nor cold nor any other enemy should rout me. Jap, I am going to make Bloomtown a real town yet. My boy, that blue calico lady was Mrs. Kelly Jones."

The grave of Benjamin Franklin and Deborah Franklin in Philadelphia. Wood engraving.. (Wellcome Collection)

BENJAMIN FRANKLIN

As an inventor, politician, philanthropist, scientist, businessman and one of our Founding Fathers, Benjamin Franklin made extraordinary contributions to humanity during his eighty-four years on the planet. Among them was Poor Richard's Almanack, in which he wrote many aphorisms, such as:

- *There are no pains without gains.*
- *Love your neighbor, yet don't pull down your hedge.*
- *Hear no ill of a friend, nor speak any of an enemy.*

When Franklin passed away in 1790, it meant the end of his inventions. No more big ideas. No more clever aphorisms. But according to S.G. Horn's 1896 book, The Next World Interviewed, Franklin wasn't quite done. His responses to a medium's question arrived in a series of aphorisms.

Of course, there were plenty of times when Franklin's ghost spoke without confining itself to short, pithy statements. In fact, one of the earliest spirit messages delivered by a medium came from Franklin on February 20, 1850, in Rochester:

> "There will be great changes in the nineteenth century. Things that now look dark and mysterious to you will be laid plain before your sight. Mysteries are going to be revealed. The world will be enlightened."

According to other mediums, he continued to speak from the Spirit world about such topics as inventions and liberty—the latter having been recorded on the "psycho-phone."

APHORISMS FROM THE AFTERLIFE

Mr. Burns, the Publisher, wrote from England to the Medium, residing in Paris, asking if she could induce the spirit of Benjamin Franklin, who had introduced Modern Spiritualism to the world, to inform the public why so many mediums were detected in fraud, and why such good mediums as the Davenport Brothers had degenerated into exhibitors of the phenomena, at the same time renouncing the truths they had once fostered. Franklin appeared—a genial, whole-souled spirit,—but would only answer his questions by the following aphorisms, in which we hope the riddle will be expounded to the reader.

It is a well-known axiom, that fraud engenders fraud.

The psychic force of a determined doubter calls up lying spirits.

Go to a spirit-circle, determined to catch the medium at fraud, and at that very seance the most reliable medium will act like the "devil."

Have the faith Christ had, and spirits will materialize in your pulpits and reading-desks. Doubt them, and they will throw bells and tambourines at you, and say the mediums did it.

The whole Arcana of Nature, spiritual and material, can be opened by the man who seeks, with patient investigation, to penetrate its mysteries.

Spiritual knowledge, like gems hidden in the bowels of the earth, is only to be reached by patient upturning of the soil.

Do not attempt a spiritual friendship with spirits who would degrade you morally or spiritually. A man is known by the company he selects, and mediums who fraternize with the spirits of Arabian mountebanks and Egyptian jugglers, should be received as exhibiting amusing phenomena, which will demonstrate spiritual truths, only as a trickish monkey demonstrates the origin of man.

The spirit who shouts your name through a trumpet, and greets you familiarly, may tickle your vanity, but cannot convey to your mind grand thoughts, or prepare you for nobler life in the Spirit Spheres.

Spirits are the souls of humanity. Among them are charlatans, beggars, murderers, thieves, simpletons, mingled with good and pure souls: intelligent, loyal, honest, and sympathetic beings.

Do not be discouraged when you find your pet medium to be a *fraud*: there have been false prophets in all ages of the world.

"Fret not thyself because of evil doers," has been the prayer of aspirants after spiritual truths, from time immemorial.

No man can navigate the air in a child's boat. To navigate the spiritual heavens requires also the appliances of science.

Franklin's kite and key unlocked the electric vaults of heaven, started the Rochester knockings, revealed the electric telegraph and telephone, and will discover the secrets of Life, Death, and Immortality.

It has taken a hundred years to develop the electric telegraph. Give us a hundred years to develop our spirit mediums.

The spirit who takes off the medium's coat, while his hands are tied behind him, is likely to be a Chinese or Hindoo juggler, who, though he perform a feat of legerdemain, should not be received as a guide in spiritual or moral affairs.

The great statesmen and thinkers, who have passed from earth, do not entertain themselves by performing curious tricks to amuse and awaken the wonder of mankind.

Into the Spirit-world are poured daily hordes of wild spirits from Asia, Africa, and Europe: the fanatics of India, the savages of the forest, the murderers, drunkards, and half-idiots that swarm the earth. Receive each according to his degree, and do not form a spiritual friendship with those who would tempt you to drink, swear, or act untruthfully.

Accept pure and noble teachings, though they come from an ignoble source, as the thirsty traveller drinks fresh, pure water from a dirty cup. Remember that a golden vessel may contain rank poison.

Truths never change though they may assume a new garment, and the manifestation of them alter. The imperfect likeness, fastened by Daguerre on a sensitive plate, foreshadowed the accurate portrait of to-day.

Crude experiments only prove the possibilities of future developments. Had you a lens powerful enough, you could see your face repeated billions of miles in space. So are truths repeated and handed down through the long ages from Spirit Spheres. So in spiritual science, the ugly, distorted image produced to-day will be superseded by the clear photograph in the future.

You cannot force the heavens, by a storm of artillery, to hearken to your prayers. Speak to Nature in her own language, and she will listen to you.

Hashesh and opium-eating produce a low form of spiritual trance, and introduce the unfortunate indulger into the degraded dens of spiritual society.

It may be optional with you whether you communicate with spirits by means of a medium or not, but it is a law of life that they should attend and influence you. On your own actions and culture depend the class of spirits who attend you.

By shutting your eyes you cannot prevent the sunlight from warming you, neither by denouncing Spiritualism can you prevent spirits from influencing you.

He who will only be fed by fairy tales in spiritual matters, will find the "Spirit-Bride,"—who treats him to a curl of her golden locks, and spins out fine meshes of lace before his wondering eyes, drawing out of space yard after yard of the cobweb texture,—is only a human syren with mask and wig, "a counterfeit presentment" of some spirit Aspasia.

Praise John, a schoolboy, for turning out his toes, and all the boys will imitate John, and cry—"We turn out our toes, too." Praise a spirit for talking through a trumpet, playing on a banjo, or showing a ghostly face through a cabinet window, and the mediums who assisted at the seance will feel—"I can do that, too"; and will, the next time, imitate the reality.

Go to hear a famous opera-singer, and you will return home humming the air, and think the tones of your voice sound quite like the prima donna's. A medium discovers within himself a power of reading names written upon paper pellets, heaped together promiscuously. That gift attracts a wondering crowd; straightway his vanity is roused, and he feels: I did that wonderful thing myself, no spirits about it Next time, he decoys a paper and reads the name himself, then confesses! *Exit.*

In the Christian Church it is said of a man, once a member, who degenerates, that "He has *fallen from grace.*" How many a poor medium falls from grace. Unable to withstand the flattery of the world, he simulates the great gifts that at first were genuine, and becoming a fraud in the eyes of the public, ends as a sham, failing to distinguish the false from the real.

A man who would go wrong under the noble teachings of *Spiritualism*, would have gone wrong, as Judas, under the pure teachings of *Christ.*

If we extol Christ's example because he was a God, how much more should we admire it as he was a *man.*

All the possibilities of Heaven and Hell are incarnate in man, as the octave embodies the grandest musical compositions for a full orchestra.

ON INVENTION

MEN have found electricity a powerful agent in the earth, but its power is not yet fully developed; spirits that gave the subject their attention while in the body, cease not their interest in it, when the body is laid by, but they continue their investigations, and assist others that come after. Let no man claim that he has made great improvements in the arts and sciences, unassisted by spirit friends. The telegraph wires would not now be conveying intelligence from one end of the land to the other, but for the assistance of disembodied spirits. We take great interest in the discoveries of science, and assist, as we find one devoted, to carry forward that which we delighted in while inhabitants of earth. But I must not dwell on any one subject, for I could fill volumes instead of a few pages. A few brief remarks may give the reader such ideas of his own powers, and the facility for acquiring knowledge, that a new world will be opened to his view, when he comes to realise, to a certainty, that he has but just entered upon a life that must surely continue without the possibility of a cessation, and according as he spends his introduction, that is, his embodied life, will his spirit life be inclined; if that has been usefully employed, and honestly devoted to elevated pursuits, the affections placed on ennobling objects, desires chaste, love pure; all these continue to grow in the continued life.

Spirit life would be tiresome, without employment; then there is nothing contrary to God's eternal and immutable laws, for man to love the pursuit most, that he preferred in the body, and he continues it providing it is useful. Thus I have continued my experiments in my present abode, and have assisted those that have been instrumental in carrying forward plans of great usefulness to man, and I tire not. To be sure my time is not wholly employed in the pursuit of any one object, but the book of nature is too vast, to be exhausted. Something new and interesting rises up before the pure mind continually, so that we do not grow weary by day, nor faint in the night seasons, but our time passes without regret, as we use it to the best advantage.

PSYCHO-PHONE MESSAGES

RECORDED BY
FRANCIS GRIERSON

Spiritual Messages from the late General U. S. Grant, on Adequate Preparation in America; Thomas Jefferson, on the Future of American Democracy; Benjamin Disraeli, on English and Irish Affairs; Prince Bismarck, on the Indemnities; John Marshall, on the Psychology of the Supreme Court of the United States; Alexander Hamilton, on the Forces that Precede Revolution; Abraham Lincoln, on the Future of Mexico; Robert Ingersoll, on Our Great Women; Henry Ward Beecher, on the New Puritanism; Benjamin Wade, of Ohio, on President Harding; General B. H. Grierson, on Japan, Mexico and California, etc.

ON LIBERTY

There is but one mark of patriotism and that is vigilance and enthusiasm. The cause of your trouble is the sincerity with which your foes think and act and the lukewarm sentiment shown by Americans, The reason is to be found in the comfort and luxury of the present day compared with the pioneer sacrifices of your fathers and grandfathers. Your opponents are vindictive as well as vigilant. They mean what they say and do what they Will. They are working as individuals, as well as in groups and parties, but Americans who inherited the land with liberty are exchanging both for the license of the maw.

When school teachers and farm hands are permitted to leave the country for the city, the end is not so far off as your sophisticated solons of the State Capitols would lead you to suppose.

I once stated that three movings equal one fire, and I can say now that the lack of teachers and farm hands has resulted in a damage equal to one revolution. No calamity comes and goes single handed. The world, the flesh and the devil are a triumvirate bound together by ties of consanguinity. Your school teachers are passing over to the world, your farm laborers to the flesh, and your ministers to the devil.

You are browsing on the stubble. One delinquency involves another, and eventually the monetary capital of the nation may be reduced to that of France. The nation will awake one day to the disillusioning fact that peace and progress cannot be gauged by commercial prosperity alone. For without food what avails your steel, your oil and your gold?

If you could witness the mortification poor Andrew Carnegie is now undergoing because of his lack of vision, you would have a lesson not soon forgotten. He built libraries but furnished no books to fill them. It was like building houses without windows. When leading business men commit such folly what can you expect of the nation at large?

The three things most needed by the people are food, raiment and shelter. The next three are instruction, religion and discipline. Liberty is a privilege; it comes after all the others. The individual has no rights inimical to those of the collective conscience.

Until you learn this fundamental maxim, all your knowledge will prove but a sounding brass and a tinkling cymbal.

The nations are rattling over the cobble stones of bankruptcy on a buckboard of compromise, on the high road to revolution.

*Washington Irving, as engraved by Hatch & Smillie.
Printed by C. R. Leslie R. A. (Public domain)*

WASHINGTON IRVING

The Legend of Sleepy Hollow, *featuring the Headless Horseman, is regarded as one of America's first, and best, ghost stories. The Horseman was inspired by tales told in the area by Dutch settlers who once found the headless corpse of a Hessian soldier—his head apparently removed by a cannonball. Legend said appearances of the Hessian's ghost were most frequent when the harvest moon was full in the sky and the pumpkins lay golden and yellow. Irving, who is considered the country's first professional writer, wrote other lesser-known ghost stories as well, such as* The Grand Prior of San Minorca *and* The Guests from Gibbet Island. *That he should later reach out to mediums from the spirit world seems perfectly fitting.*

In the writing that follows, Irving's spirit describes his travels in a swan-shaped electric chariot en route to the home of former Speaker of the House, Henry Clay, where he meets with many of his old friends and peers, including Benjamin Franklin and George Washington.

VISIT TO HENRY CLAY

HAVING recovered my health after a sojourn of two weeks amid the charming scenery of Mount Rosalia, or the "Rose-colored Mount," I set forth one morning, accompanied by a competent guide, to visit the home of my friend, Henry Clay. The morning was uncommonly fine, even for the sweet Land of the Blest, and the fragrance from the roses blooming upon the hill-side was fairly intoxicating.

Our phaeton was a small, white, swan-shaped carriage, ornamented with golden designs, and propelled by a galvanic battery in the graceful swan-head, which at my request took the place of the ordinary steed.

This was, to me, an exceedingly novel mode of travel, which my short sojourn in the spirit world had prevented me from before enjoying.

We glided over the electric ground with the speed of lightning and smooth harmony of music. The road over which we rolled was white and lustrous as parian marble, and adorned on either side with most rare and beautiful forms of foliage; ever and anon we passed gay cavalcades and bands of spirits, who were evidently, from their festal garments, and the bright emanations which they diffused through the air, bound for some harmonial gathering on one of the numerous islands which dot the sparkling river Washingtonia, so named after George Washington.

The distance from the point whence I started, according to earth's computation, was over one hundred miles; but though I desired my guide to move onward as slowly as possible, that I might enjoy the prospect before me, we reached our destination in less than a quarter of an hour!

I had received a special invitation from Henry Clay to visit him on this occasion, as he had called together some choice friends to give me welcome; yet, although I knew I was expected, my surprise cannot be described upon beholding the air filled with bevies of beautiful ladies, like radiant birds, approaching, with the sound of music and flutter of flowers, to receive me. Thus surrounded and escorted, I was borne to the noble palace (for such it may be justly termed) of Henry Clay.

AFTERLIFESYLES OF THE RICH AND FAMOUS

The structure is of white alabaster, faced with a pale yellow semi-transparent stone, which glistened most gorgeously. The form of the building is unlike any order of architecture with which I had been acquainted. The avenue by which it was approached was decorated alternately with statues of representative Americans, and a peculiar flowering tree, whose green leaves and yellow blossoms, of gossamer texture, resembled the fine mist of a summer morning. Terminating, this avenue was the main entrance, surmounted by the grand dome of the edifice. In the rear of this rotunda, extending on either side, appeared the main building, rising, turret on turret, like a stupendous mountain of alabaster beaming as with soft moonlight in the clear summer air.

We entered by ascending a staircase composed of twelve broad steps. And here let me pause, before recounting my interview with the celebrated statesman, to describe the main hall, whose magnificence I, upon entering, hastily surveyed, but which I afterward studied more completely. The floor of this hall was formed of delicate cerulean blue gems. From its centre sprang, like a fountain, a most wonderful representation of a flowering plant resembling the lotus, composed of precious and brilliant stones. The green leaves forming the base were of transparent emerald, and the white lily which surmounted the stem blossomed out clearer than any crystal. The yellow centre, corresponding to the pistils, formed a divan. This beautiful ornament was intended for the desk of the orator. The dome, which was several hundred feet high, was open to the summer sky, and arranged in tiers graduated one above the other. The lower tier was filled with paintings indicating the progress of the United States of America. Surmounting this was a gallery of small compartments, each hung with silver and gold gauze drapery, and similar in construction to the boxes of a theatre; these opened into halls or alleys leading to private apartments connecting with the main building. Above these boxes were placed artistically-carved animals, representing the native beasts of America. Above these again, appeared groups in marble of the fruits of the country. No sooner had I entered the building which I have been describing, than a peculiar rushing sound like distant music reached my ear; on lifting my eyes in the direction of the sound, I beheld descending through the air the majestic form of Henry Clay. He approached with extended hand and fascinating smile to receive me. How like and yet how unlike the famous man I had known on earth! The gray hair of age had given place to the abundant glossy locks of youth. The intellectual eye beamed with a new life and his whole person sent forth an effulgence most attractive. Those of my readers who knew him on earth will well remember the peculiar fascination of his sphere, but they can form from the remembrance but a slight idea of the attractive aura he sheds forth in this existence. I immediately felt myself drawn by an invisible power toward him. He grasped my hand with the frank cordiality and grace of former days, and leading me thus, we arose together and, passing through one of the arched compartments of the upper tier, entered another portion of the building. As we moved on I seemed to live portions of my earthly life, long past. The gorgeous and fantastic architecture which everywhere met my eye reminded me of the halls of the Alhambra. Swiftly passing, we emerged through a spacious arch upon an open arbor, where were congregated the priests whom I had been invited to meet. I started back with a shock of delight when I beheld, in the centre of the group, the immortal figure of George Washington. I knew him instantly, partly from the likenesses which had been extant on earth, and partly from the noble spirit which emanated like a sun from his person. The group parted as we entered and I immediately felt, resting upon my shoulder like a benediction, the soft, firm hand of the Father of his Country. "Washington!" I exclaimed, fervidly grasping his hand. "At length we have met!" he responded, and a smile of ineffable joy lighted his countenance. He then spoke of the many changes through which the United States had passed since his removal to the spirit land. I was surprised at the extent of knowledge he displayed. Not the slightest variation in the scale of political economy had escaped his notice. He expressed himself pleased especially at the great progress and development of the people within the last twenty years. He alluded to their rapid march through the western territories; the founding of new and important States; the development of the agricultural and mineral resources of countries supposed to be almost valueless; of the invention and construction of machinery adapted to the wants and necessities of those new and rapidly-increasing States. "This marvellous growth is owing to their being essentially a mediumistic people—is it not so?" said he, smiling and turning to the assembled guests. "Yes, yes!" I heard repeated on all sides. On this commenced a general conversation. I listened as one in a dream. Around me I beheld the faces and forms of the heroes of past history, each bearing the shape and semblance of humanity, though removed from earth millions of miles into space. One and all emitted, like stars, their own peculiar luminous aura. Collected in motley groups were Benjamin Franklin, John Hancock, William Penn, Old General Jackson, John Jacob Astor, De Witt Clinton, and many of the old Knickerbocker residents of New York; with Sir Robert Peel, Lord Brougham, the Duke of Wellington, Hunt, Keats, Byron, Scott, Cowper, Hume, Goethe, De Stael, Mrs. Hemans, and many others.

"The people of America have progressed to an astonishing degree," said a musical voice at my left. "We must initiate Irving into the means by which we impart knowledge to the mediumistic nation through the Cabinet at Washington."

"Certainly," responded Henry Clay. "Let all formalities cease. We will partake of refreshments, and then Franklin will make him acquainted with the wonderful aids to science and humanity with which he has supplied my residence."

As he ceased speaking, a shower of sound, like the music from the ringing of innumerable crystal bells, filled the air. Accompanying this, and apparently descending from the ceiling, a soft light of aromatic odor diffused itself through the apartment. This was followed by the appearance of a shining disk of amber and pearl, revolving rapidly in its descent till it reached the congregated party. This magic circle (which Thomas Hood, who was present, facetiously termed the "wheel of fortune") was supplied with refreshments truly supernal. Here were fruits of most brilliant dyes; some of soft, pulpy flesh, and others of the consistency of honey; some more transparent than the diamonds of earth; others substantial, seemingly intended to supply the demands of hunger. Here were confections resembling foam and cloud, whose very taste was elysium. The guests ate and chatted vivaciously. I received much information concerning the various products of this great land which were displayed upon the table. The most luscious fruits, I considered, both in flavor and quality, were those produced on an island in the spirit land corresponding to your island of Cuba, which was under the protection of a band of spirits called the "Good Sisters."

The company having regaled themselves at the table, arose and divided into groups, laughing and chatting like ordinary mortals. I felt immediately attracted to a cluster of which Benjamin Franklin was the magnetic centre. I reminded him of the duties imposed on him by our host, and told him playfully that I desired to investigate the mysteries of this wonderful palace. He cordially acquiesced, and, in company with a few friends, we commenced our explorations. I inquired as to the construction of the table from which we had just arisen, so superior to the cumbersome ones of earth. "It is a very simple contrivance," he smilingly remarked. "You observe inserted in these twisted columns, ornamented with leaves, which support the ceiling, an electric wire, similar to that of a telegraph. From each of these central columns, this wire connects with the upper gallery. Here," said he, pointing to one of the leafy ornaments, "you perceive the means of communicating. Unobserved by you, our gracious host touched one of these springs which are connected with the crystal bells, and announced to his servants his desire for refreshments." "Servants!" exclaimed I. "How singular! I little supposed, from the religious teachings I had received, that there would be menials in heaven!"

"Thee has a poor memory," remarked William Penn, with a bright smile, "Did not the Bible teach thee that there was an upper and a lower seat? These servants are composed mostly of those who were held in slavery on earth and who desire to receive instruction that they may progress in the spheres. They are willing assistants; giving, that they may receive in return. If thee dislike the term 'servant,' thee may use the term 'friend,' for they are friends and co-workers. Through those doors in the gallery they bring the refreshments which they gather from the hanging gardens without, where they live like the Peries of the East. The luxury of the princes of earth cannot compare with the life of enjoyment and freedom led by those whom I have termed 'servants.'"

I here took the opportunity to ask Franklin if it was necessary, in communicating with absent individuals, to use those external appliances? "Not always; thought can commune with thought if upon the same plane; but a mind like that of our great statesman cannot readily communicate with one whose mind on earth never rose above the domestic affairs of life. In such cases, external means are necessary."

"Come," said he, turning; "I will show you something more remarkable than this." So saying, he led me through an open door into one of the spacious gardens which grace the palace on either side. We walked but a few moments, arm in arm, over a soft velvet like lawn, of the color of a delicate violet. Exquisite tints everywhere met my eye. The air was like wine, and so luscious and entrancing were the surroundings that I felt inclined to tarry, but my sage guide, calling my attention to the majestic dome towering in the air, desired me to exert my will to ascend. I did so, and immediately felt myself rising as if pressed up by some elastic substance, until I reached the top. The dome, which appeared to be composed of glass, I perceived, as I approached, was covered with a thin web resembling that of a spider. The apex of this dome was surmounted by a globe representing the planet earth, with its continents and seas. Openings corresponding to the different continents admitted persons into the globe. We entered that corresponding to the continent of North America. Each of these entrances, I was told, was particularly adapted to the admission of the inhabitants of the different localities they represented. On looking down I beheld the apartment I had first entered. It was no longer vacant—each gallery was filled with spectators. On the lily-shaped rostrum stood Henry Clay and George Washington—Washington speaking to the people. "You observe," said my guide, "a secondary stem from that lily branches off and extends to this point. It appears to you a mere ornament, but it transmits the thoughts and words of the speaker to the city of Washington. Other branches, as you notice, lead in other directions. If the speaker desires his thoughts to be transmitted to any given point, he leans toward the stem leading to that point. This silken web which you have admired, is a sensitive electric telegraph. It is composed of the elements of mind; in the world you have lately inhabited it would be intangible, but it has a subtle connection with the human brain, and spirit thoughts directed through it go with the promptness of electricity to their destination. Thought is electric, but its power of transmitting itself is, like that of the human voice, limited; the voice requires the artificial assistance of a speaking-trumpet to throw its sound beyond the ordinary distance; thought requires a similar artificial conductor. You remember," said Franklin, "in my early experiments with the kite and key, I could not obtain the spark until I had established the necessary attraction, although the air was filled with the electric current. So of the thought-electricity, which is constantly flowing; we have to apply means to concentrate it and give it form and expression. On earth, word and gesture are media for thought, but the savans have not yet discovered the means by which unspoken thought can take form and expression. No galvanic wire nor chemical battery has yet been invented by them, through which these electric sparks may be drawn down from their unseen habitations among the clouds; but in the world of spirits this great discovery, as I have shown you, has been made. In this appliance you find the thoughts of the speaker running through these sensitive wires until, like telegraphic messages, they reach their destination on earth."

I listened to Franklin's explanation of this gigantic sensorium with my soul filled with love and admiration for the great Creator who had formed the human mind with its vast capacity for penetrating the sublime mysteries of nature.

After leaving the dome I continued my inspection of the edifice. But of its halls and galleries, its boudoirs, libraries, and peerless gardens, I will speak at some future time.

Irving wrote of many ghosts before allegedly writing from the spirit world. This image, by Frederick Simpson Coburn, portrays Sleepy's Hollow's *Ichabod Crane imagining a phantom. (Public domain)*

Peter Cooper, photographed by Brown Brothers. (Public domain)

PETER COOPER

If you live in New York City, you might know Peter Cooper best by the places named after him: Cooper Union, Cooper Square, and Stuyvesant Town-Peter Cooper Village.

Cooper earned those honors through a lifetime of achievements as an industrialist, inventor, philanthropist, politician, and realtor. All of which made him one of New York City's richest men.

Cooper passed away in 1883 at the age of 92, but returned from the dead shortly after to chat with a medium about his passion for learning, and how the spirit world has influenced many of the greatest thinkers during their best years— the years while they were alive. Though spirits may not have actually given humankind knowledge, Cooper's ghost was right about electric cars becoming familiar all over the planet. The medium, however, likely knew that they were already in development in the 1880s, before internal combustion engines took over for the next hundred some years. The spirit also refers to an electric vehicle mentioned in a previous book the medium was associated with, Strange Visitors, *from 1869 (and included in the preceding Washington Irving section).*

EDUCATIONAL INSTITUTIONS IN THE SPIRIT-WORLD

I AM safely over, but what a strange world I have entered, widely different from any preconceptions I had formed of it, although I was somewhat familiar with Spiritualism and its teachings.

I see life everywhere about me: busy, happy life. Spirits flying to and fro on missions of love or mercy; many have a light like a sun radiating from their head and figure. One can see these lights at a great distance; shining in various colours and different degrees of magnitude. When moving toward you, and within a mile or two of where you are, the light appears to open, and you recognise in it some friend dear to you, or some individual known to you by engraving or photographic likeness, approaching to talk with you, for though it is not necessary to be near to friends to speak with them, yet spirits generally desire to be in close proximity with those they love. The telephone has been known and in use from time immemorial in the Spirit-world. The means of conveying thought among cultivated and highly developed spirits is by a mental process. Thought generates electricity, which, like lightning, conveys the idea, and photographs it on another receptive mind.

Every invention on earth that has benefitted mankind, appears to have sprung from this Spirit-world. I remember to have read, years ago, in "Strange Visitors" of a visit to Henry Clay's home, and of how he communicated with distant parts of his building by means of electric cords. That was the foreshadowing of an invention since developed on earth, which will assist in making mankind all one harmonious family.

The electrically-propelled car, by which Irving glided over the spirit roads, will shortly be familiar to all the inhabitancy of earth; they will traverse the globe as we traverse the fields of space.

I am astonished to find the number of temples of learning that exist here. I have been shewn some one-hundred times as large as the Institute I established after my humble fashion on earth. They are circular in form, or shaped like a magnet, with an outer corridor to different entrances, and an inner court, with fountains throwing up delicious essences and of invigorating perfume, while trees and strange flowering plants embellish the parks by which they are surrounded. Trees, here, are unlike earthly trees, the leaves being of variegated colours, resembling the autumnal foliage of the American forest.

When I speak of temples of learning, I do not mean mere schools for the study of arithmetic, geography, writing, &c., that appertain to the earth-plane. These Spirit-colleges are intended to develop the soul of man, and teach him his relations to mankind; to instruct him in the wonders of the sidereal heavens, impart to him knowledge of the inhabitants of the sun, moon, and stars, the numerous worlds in space occupied by various tribes of men. To aid him, also, in experimenting in chemistry and sciences, by which he can explore the uttermost extent of the universe; to instruct him in political economy and laws governing humanity, that he may develop means to ameliorate the condition of the unprogressive and helpless portion of mankind.

From these grand Spirit-universities are promulgated all the progressive doctrines that startle Christendom. All scholars and clergymen who secede from the doctrines taught by the Churches, are in spirit-communion with the leaders of these Spirit-institutions.

It was from this superior source that Shelley received his inspiration, and wrote under spirit-dictation his *Queen Mab* which, at the age of nineteen or twenty, caused his expulsion from an English college, and brought about a new era of thought. Here Theodore Parker received the light which illumined his works. Here the science of communicating with earth was first developed. From this quarter Darwin, Wallace, Varley, Crookes, Tyndall, received the ideas which have made their names famous.

From my earth-efforts to give free instruction to the youth of America, in engraving, painting, designing, and kindred arts, I have been chosen for similar work in the Spirit-world. I find enough to do here. Enormous numbers of youths arrive daily in the Spirit-spheres. Many are ignorant of all arts and sciences, and have had no opportunity to develop their mental and spiritual natures. I have formed a school to teach them how to educate their inventive and constructive talents, for the power to construct and build is God-like. The most unhappy spirits are those who are idle, and know not what to do with life; who have no idea of employing the time in useful labours. Old age is a blessing. Experience brings wisdom. I am thankful I lived as long as I did on earth. I have now commenced to grow younger, but it is the youth of a full-grown tree, renewing its leaves and sap with the spring.

Queen Victoria and a still-alive Prince Albert, Buckingham Palace, 1854. Photographed by Roger Fenton. (Public domain)

PRINCE ALBERT

Queen Victoria and her beloved husband, Prince Albert, were known to attend séances as early as 1846. So when Albert died in 1861 at just 42 years of age, the Queen was not willing to let go. Instead, she opted for a truly long-distance relationship with the help of a thirteen-year-old medium named Robert Lees, who had delivered a message from Albert that she deemed authentic. Victoria invited Lees to be her resident medium at Buckingham Palace, but he declined and instead introduced her to another medium, John Brown. Brown equally impressed the Queen and served her spiritual needs for more than thirty years—occasionally receiving messages from Albert that helped her determine political policies.

Albert, however, didn't limit himself to Brown. Other mediums channeled his spirit as well, in service of the Queen, of course. The message included here was received in December 1876. It includes comments on his continued relationship with the Queen and notes on the spirit status of past monarchs.

ENGLAND AND THE QUEEN

I LOVE England and am interested in her welfare, not as a ruler, but as an adviser and friend. I watch over the councils of the Queen, and I make one of the Cabinet. I attend Parliament, accompanied sometimes by Lords Brougham and Palmerston, and others who have made affairs of State their study in life. I have met there from time to time Pitt and Fox, the Duke of Wellington, and many more who still feel an interest in the welfare of their native land.

Personally I attend the Queen daily; so strong are her mediumistic powers, so perfect is the unison between us two, that I feel as though we had never been separated. I live as it were in two worlds!

Victoria has told the public of our happy home in the Highlands. She delights in natural, simple life, and thinks, as I do, that the ideal monarch should be one with the people, not above them.

The Queen loves Balmoral, and it is because my spirit can visit untrammeled that free mountain-place, that she is drawn thither. If the public could understand the true reason for her choice they would cease to cavil at it.

A portion of time spent among mountains helps to develop a love of freedom, and a true knowledge of the natural equality between men. Spirits also can approach mortals more intimately upon elevated ground, and it is for these reasons that the Queen loves Balmoral, and this is why the true Briton loves to explore mountain-heights.

Some of Victoria's subjects reproach her for not supporting the dignity of the nation by external show; but court pageants are merely pastimes for the ignorant, and tend to blind and subjugate the oppressed by the dazzle and splendour of pomp. A self-poised, cultivated nation should rise above mere childish glitter, and England is gradually doing this. I think the Queen is right in withdrawing from spectacles which subserve the purpose of diverting the mind from its true necessities and a rightful understanding of its condition. Time was when barbaric shows were necessary accompaniments to the triumphal chariot of the conqueror. Not that I desire to deprecate pleasure where it tends to invigorate and restore too greatly taxed energies; but a useless expenditure of wealth in pageants in the end only cripples the people, and weakens them both in body and mind.

Before our day many kings and queens reigned in England, and I have had the rare happiness of meeting several of them in spirit-life. But are they kings and queens still? No; many have learned that they were unfitted for the positions they held on earth.

But few among them possessed minds of great comprehension, a few only were able to look beyond themselves and perceive the needs of the people over whom they reigned.

Our unfortunate cousin, Charles I, lost his life because he thought only of his immediate wants, and would not listen to the requests of his people. I have met him in spirit-life an altered man.

Progress, and the development of the human race, is the law of the Universe. The Spirit-world controls the earth, it puts forth its unseen hand, and drags from the throne the potentate who would crush the people, and take from them their hard-earned pittance, or push them back into the dark caverns of ignorance.

This is the occult force that overturns nations and empires! It was this mighty spirit-power that drove Marie Antoinette to the block, and tore the triumphant eagle from the banner of Napoleon!

Unhappy Marie Antoinette! her sufferings on earth in some measure atoned for her pride of power! I have seen her in spirit-life, beautified by sorrow, educated by sad experience; living a quiet uneventful life in a tranquil home; no longer queen! no longer hated nor despised!

I have seen Mary Queen of Scots, another unfortunate queen, but possessed of a finer nature than Marie Antoinette, a loving though an erring woman. She leads a more active life of charity than the other Marie. Possessed of a strong love nature, and a subtle magnetic power, she makes herself felt both in the Spirit-world and on earth. She had no desire to oppress the people, she was merely misled by her cravings for a stronger nature than her own to sustain her, and by her desire to be loved and admired.

The two Napoleons are together in spirit-life. They are men of the people. Though temporarily blinded by power, they aimed at the uplifting of the masses. When they tightened their grip on the people, it was loosened by spirit-power, and now they are true democrats. They have many adherents in the world they inhabit, and are still leaders. Possessed of a tremendous energy, they can accomplish great good; their views are large and not self-centred; and though they keep their eye on France, they visit other nations, and study different modes of government.

This wonderful panorama of life interests me deeply. History here walks before me, not in book form, but clothed and living.

I wish to apprise persons holding responsible positions on earth, of the important fact that those who have ruled kingdoms in life cannot return to earth and communicate their thoughts more readily than those who have held the most humble position.

Death is said to be a leveler of distinctions, and such it would be if the education and information we acquire on earth did not accompany us to the second stage of existence.

Be a man a king or a commoner, if he educates his mind and develops his moral faculties, he will reap the benefit of his earth efforts in the after state. Such has been my happy experience. I rejoice that I gave my attention to belles-lettres, the study of the fine arts, and political economy, and that I used my efforts to advocate the welfare of the people over whom Victoria reigned.

In thus educating my mind and elevating my soul, I prepared myself for an equable enjoyment in the spirit-world. My acquirements have aided me here; the sentiments of faith and trust in a Supreme Power, and the love of humanity which my Consort's true womanly nature fostered, have aided me in securing employment for my faculties in this Land of Immortality! Though this is a world of light and beauty, old associations live actively within my breast, and family ties survive the dissolution of the material body, therefore I pass much of my time in dear old England.

I have before said, if a ruler ceases to look after the interests of the masses—if he forgets that he is placed in power as a guide and father to his subjects— if he forgets these things, he will sooner or later be hurled from his throne, and uprooted from the ground which seems to him so firm.

The step of Justice seems slow in reaching some nations, while it overtakes others with rapidity, but though it be retarded for a time, it cannot be evaded. Already has it reached the Papal dominions; its tread is now shaking the throne of the Ottoman empire! Wherever there is oppression—wherever there is an attempt to stay the hand of Progress and enforce ignorance—there will Justice appear in the form of revolution and war; it is foreordained.

In America your rulers hold a short-lived power; but as true as there is any attempt to oppress the poor, to withhold the influence of public schools and universal education, to draw from any portion of the inhabitants their just prerogatives, or to oppress in any way the masses, you will feel the influence of that spirit-power, which regulates governments and the kingdoms of earth, rebuking and leading you through darkness to a higher form of government!

Emanuel Swedenborg. (Wellcome Collection)

EMANUEL SWEDENBORG

Early in his life Swedish inventor and scientist Emanuel Swedenborg was known for his expertise in engineering, geometry, chemistry, metallurgy, anatomy, and physiology. But by his fifties, having mastered the natural sciences and the physical world, he decided to pivot to the spiritual side. Swedenborg began having out-of-body experiences and receiving messages about the universe and its planets from angels. He detailed this newfound information in several books, including Heaven and Its Wonders and Hell from Things Heard and Seen *and* Earths in Our Solar System Which Are Called Planets, and Earths in the Starry Heaven Their Inhabitants, and the Spirits and Angels There. *The spirits of Mars, in his opinion, are "among the best of all spirits who come from the earths of this solar system."*

Swedenborg was a Spiritualist before anyone was calling it Spiritualism. His experiences and writings even inspired a set of followers calling themselves Swedenborgians. Followers or not, mediums jumped on this pioneer's bandwagon and claimed to have received his messages from the Other Side. In the following letter, which Swedenborg's spirit dated August 13, 1851, he offers a few new learnings to the living. Decades later another medium received a series of letters, two of which are reproduced here and profess that the books he'd written about the spirits were misinformed.

MAGNETISM AND COMMUNICATION

MY DEAR FRIEND:

I am rejoiced to meet you, and will now allude to the subject of magnetism, one not generally appreciated.

It is as much under the control of laws, as any of the attributes that belong to man's nature, but how little understood, indeed, at the time of my bodily life. I knew not that there was such an agent in the frame of man, and yet I was more subject to its influence than any I was acquainted with. By its influence, the sick may de healed, the troubled mind hushed into peace, and the peaceful mind troubled. Hence, that which is so powerful for good or for evil, should be better understood.

Much advantage will be derived from this manner of communicating. The separation of the two spheres is almost annihilated, besides other evidences I saw as I approached you—that you was conversing with your guardian spirit, apparently, in as familiar a manner as though you saw each other.

To be sure you could not see each other, but she readily read the questions as they assumed a form in your mind, and proceeded to answer them with a pen in your hand. What greater evidence can be desired than this, of there being an intelligence which reads your most secret thoughts, and moves the pen.

My friend, I desire you to continue to cherish the idea that good spirits will never teach falsehood, but will always endeavor to elevate their friends both in their present and future condition.—This is as true as any law that is established by God—as immutable and unchangeable as himself.

We find ourselves here in a condition so far above our highest desires, that language would fail me to even faintly portray it.

As I had often the privilege of conversing with spirits, I supposed that I had a pretty correct idea of my future home. But not so. I was lost in wonder when I entered my new life, where l had a new body formed. I was delighted with my change.—At first I could scarcely realize that it was myself, I looked for my hands, and there they were, I looked for my feet, and they too were there; and so of every part of my body, nothing was lacking.

I cast a view at my old frame, that had done me good service heretofore, it now seemed too worth less to be concerned about, I saw my friends with sadness in their countenances, moving gently about as though afraid of waking me. Could I have spoken, I would have said, Only put it where it will not annoy you. I am as really with you as when I moved that body about. I found myself welcomed to my new home by congenial spirits, and such a welcome no man can fully realise until he leaves his cumberous body. My new associates led me off to a view of distant objects, and to try my new body. I found that space was nearly annihilated—we moved with that speed of which you can conceive an idea off, by thinking of the magnetic telegraph, My first journey was to visit a planet; it was delightful to pass thus as easy, as I formerly did to a neighbors. I then returned to earth to see how my friends were managing with my former body, I was present at the funeral.

I felt a desire to speak out the words with which my mind was filled, I would gladly have told them that I was in their midst, the minister should have known this or not undertaken to teach spiritual knowledge. I have much to say; I want to speak of the condition of other spirits, but time fails. I must leave you with thanks for your kindness.

— EMANUEL SWEDENBORG

A SELF-RETRACTION

June 22, 1882

In my philosophy of correspondences there was much truth, with here and there a shade of error. It was argumentative, speculative, and characterized by analagous reasoning, but not sufficiently intuitive to reach the full height of spiritual induction. But whatever errors may have crept into this department of my writings, they have been comparatively harmless.

What has given me the greatest annoyance since my departure from the flesh, or rather since I have better understood the subject; and what has given me the greatest anxiety to have eradicated from the minds of those who read me believingly, are my teachings on the subject of the hells in the spiritual world. I desire here to lay down a proposition I know to be true, whoever may state to the contrary, namely: 'No embodied spirit was ever enabled, no matter how highly developed the organism of the subject, to leave the body, go into the spiritual spheres, undergo experiences there, behold scenes, hold converse with their inhabitants, witness events and occurrences transpiring there, then return to the body, bring it back into normal action, and then correctly and in detail and in purity of narrative give to the world through the physical organism of the body, what it had seen, heard, and witnessed,' during its temporary absence. If it were otherwise, and the spiritual world a real, fixed and objective reality, all who visited it in spirit during physical embodiment, would on returning and reanimating the body with the returning spiritual influx impart the same information and recite the same story. The directly opposite of this is true, and settles the question irrevocably in the negative as to the absolute reliability of knowledge imparted by spirits while inhabiting the natural body, although permitted by the operation of a certain law which is neither wholly spiritual nor physical, but a combination of both, to leave for a short period its tenement of flesh. Even then the spirit entire does not vacate the body, even for an instant of time, for if it did life in the body would become immediately extinct. However far the consciousness of the spirit may wander away from its home in the material house it must maintain an inseparable connection with it, at least by a portion of the magnetism of itself. Therefore during its visits away it is nevertheless all the while connected with the body, and hampered and fettered by it, and more or less governed by its laws and conditions. It can not, therefore, on returning, and it has never been wholly absent, give fully, purely, and correctly its spiritual observations and experiences.

When I visited the spiritual world during my embodied life I was governed by this same law and subjected to the same limitations, and hence what I related was not entitled to full credence and belief. So it has been in all cases of trance in the past, and will continue to be in the future for ages yet to come.

— EMANUEL SWEDENBORG

June 29, 1882

Since I have been inducted into higher light and blessed with the true knowledge I have been utterly amazed in reviewing my writings, resulting in the discovery of two facts, namely, their prolixity in matter and stupendousness in folly. It seems to me now as almost utterly incredible that in my efforts at the spiritual interpretation of the scriptures I should have written so many absolutely silly and unmeaning things. It becomes my duty, and I can not be happy without it, to make this declaration, however humiliating it may be to me, viewed from your standpoint, but the truth and the peace, happiness and progress of my spirit require it. No work was ever written but what an ingenious metaphysician might not twist out of its every paragraph an assumed interior and mysterious meaning.

— EMANUEL SWEDENBORG

HEAVEN ON MARS

Once a spirit has left Earth it has access to the great vastness of, well, anywhere that's not Earth. According to several late nineteenth-century mediums, and before them, Emanuel Swedenborg, that includes Mars.

Swedenborg claimed to have left his body and visited our interplanetary neighbor. There, he discovered a race of Martians living in peaceful civilizations with no system of government.

More than a century later, a Swiss medium named Hélène Smith began falling into trances and taking her own spiritualistic visits to Mars. The Red Planet, she said, was filled with wonders, including carriages that glided by without horses or wheels, houses with fountains on their roofs, and at least one very strange two-foot-long beast sporting a flat tail, the "head of a cabbage" with a big green eye in the middle, six paws, and many ears. Smith even learned to speak and write in Martian.

This section, however, features just one tale of Mars, delivered to the medium, Lizzie S. Green, by the spirit of Madam Fredrika Ehrenborg. Erhenborg was born in 1794 in Sweden, just twenty-two years after Swedenborg's death. She found herself greatly inspired by his works and became an ardent Swedenborgian, even writing books and pamphlets to promote the movement. Her spirit left her body in 1873, and allegedly drifted all the way to Mars.

Madam Ehrenborg's experiences and observations, as recorded by Green and published in A Book Written by the Spirits of the So-Called Dead, *follow in their entirety.*

A BOOK

WRITTEN BY THE

SPIRITS OF THE SO-CALLED DEAD,

WITH THEIR OWN MATERIALIZED HANDS, BY THE
PROCESS OF INDEPENDENT SLATE-WRITING,

THROUGH

MRS. LIZZIE S. GREEN AND OTHERS,

AS MEDIUMS.

COMPILED AND ARRANGED BY

C. G. HELLEBERG,

OF CINCINNATI, OHIO.

Life is real! life is earnest!
And the grave is not its goal;
Dust thou art, to dust returnest,
Was not written of the soul.
—LONGFELLOW.

CINCINNATI:
1883.

DESCRIPTION OF THE JOURNEY TO MARS, AND WONDERFUL INFORMATION FURNISHED BY MADAM EHRENBORG

March 9, 1882—Our party of tourists, after having been carefully selected in accordance with their ability to utilize the magnetic currents that connect the planets in our solar system, and their adaptability to the electric and magnetic condition of Mars, whither we were bound, started on the journey at, according to your time, midnight, February 23. We proceeded without any incident of note until we reached Maluka Plains, where we met a party of excursionists on a visit to our planet earth. Maluka Plains, named after a great prophet of Mars, are located many millions of miles from the circling magnetic belts of earth, and immediately adjacent to the outer circle of the electro-magnetic atmosphere of Mars. We were surprised to find that these excursionists were acquainted with our guide and leader, Mr. Swedenborg, for he had frequently visited the most interesting points of our stellar system. He had even been at Mars in spirit while he was in the body of flesh, but he finds many things quite different from what he thought he had discovered during his spiritual visits when embodied. The party we met were on a tour of scientific exploration, and gladly availed themselves of information imparted by Swedenborg and Polheim, and we in return were greatly aided by data and information furnished by them to us. While this conference, or rather exchange of information, was in progress a courier was dispatched by our newly-made acquaintances to the spiritual magnates of Mars concerning our coming. I shall here stop and defer a description of our first reception until our next sitting.

March 13—As we entered within the magnetic radius of Mars, and were emerging from the outer into the inner concentric circles, so characteristic of that planet, we met a reception committee of several thousand, and after formal greetings, we were escorted to a magnificent edifice, where were in waiting innumerable throngs of spiritual dignitaries and others to receive us. I here desire to remark that in my use of words I resort to your own vocabulary, for the thought language of the Marsians is quite different from the sound of your words, and to employ their terms would only confound you and militate against your proper conception and understanding of the narrative. For instance, I use the word edifice to indicate a structure, but they use an entirely different term and form of expression, and so on ad infinitum. The edifice referred to I am unable to describe, and it can only be fully understood in thought. In dimensions so great that your city of Cincinnati could be settled in one corner of it without attracting but very little attention. The material of which it is composed has no fitting representative on earth in its present state of development. Your diamonds and precious stones are as dim and unreflecting in comparison as a cloudy, murky day of autumn is to a bright summer day with the sun at meridian and the horizon unobstructed by cloud or a single mist. This comparison may serve to give you some idea of the absorbingly intense brilliancy of the mammoth structure, yet this is of itself but as a mote in the sunbeam to what I am assured exists in the immeasurable immensity of the higher creations in the inconceivable and boundless universe of God. Oh, how diminutive is this little ball of matter called earth, when we only measurably take in the vast immensity of the infinite domain of God. And poor, puny man, what a mere speck—a mere infinitisimal animalcule. As we approached this mammoth structure, it seemed to be tremulous with motion, and the motion, superinduced by such intensely penetrating, soul dazzling strains of music as to perfectly appal with ecstatic emotion our enraptured tourists. But for the preparation of us for it by the scientific spirits, who they called the Ulaetta, we could not have withstood it. I will give you this process of preparation on some future occasion, and I am sure it will be interesting to you and valuable when you come over. The ceremonies of reception were performed, not in speech, but in musical opera, which, singular to state, we were enabled to understand by the preparation mentioned. When I say musical opera I do not mean singing accompanied by music, but that the music itself was intensely operatic, and infused thought by the most astonishing and utterly inexplicable process into our interior soul consciousness. It was something worth years of suffering and pain to enjoy, and in contemplating its inconceivable grandeur I return to my own sphere, feeling how little I am, and to weep for the children of earth, still in ignorance and superstition, and I lift my voice in prayerful supplication to God to rend the veil, that poor humanity may obtain even faint glimpses of the gorgeous splendors of God's great kingdom; but I seem to hear a voice answering, Not yet; wait and be patient.

March 20—We observed the most singular fact connected with the edifice wherein we were received. In approaching it we were unable to penetrate into its interior with our vision. It seemed to be a solid mass of exquisitely fine material, but on gaining admission into its interior, by some peculiar power that seemed to affect our spiritual vision and perceptions, we were enabled to see through and beyond it, and to perceive objects in the far distance. In other words, the whole structure seemed to vanish so far as to permit no obstruction to our vision far beyond its limits, and yet it was thoroughly substantial, composed of finely attenuated and spiritually sublimated material. I have so much to tell you that I must forego the pleasure of indulging in details, however interesting they might be to you.

The presiding personage at our reception was a figure of tall and commanding appearance, with a benevolent face, dignified mien, and large blue eyes, that seemed constantly tremulous with love and emotion. He held in his hand a magic wand, which ever and anon he would wave, and in harmony with these movements the most enchanting sounds of music seemed to be wafted far out in the viewless spiritual ether that surrounded and enveloped us. This wonderful fact baffles the skill of mortal pen and mortal language to describe, and you must be content with what is said as the best that can be said, so as to reach your comprehension.

As I caught the eye of this great presiding spirit I perceived the idea emanating from his mind, 'I am glad to meet you,' yet not one of these words was spoken. I essayed to answer to express my thankfulness for his friendly recognition of us, and I found I could not speak audibly, but my thought he caught immediately, and bowed in acknowledgment. He had been many thousands of years before a sage and philosopher on the planet Mars, and bore about the same relation to his people as Mahomet, Confucius, Jesus, Swedenborg and others of their day have in your world; and he is pre-eminent in music. All the great spirits of Mars are eminent musicians. Music, intellectual expansion and spiritual growth seem to be wedded, and go hand in hand together. These are wonderful relations, but nevertheless are true.

In my next I will introduce you to some of the societies and cities of the planet, to be followed from time to time by revelations that can not fail to impress you with the greatest interest, and not only be interesting and instructive, but will be of great value to you in your after life in the spheres. My clear and venerable friend, be of good cheer, and in the sweet bye and bye I will accompany you on this very tour, and then you will perceive the difficulties in the way of giving a description so as to be understood by mortals.

March 27—After the ceremonies of reception, the details of which, fully set forth, would fill a large volume, we set out under the escort of a select delegation of forty-seven in number on a tour of inspection, a few only of the incidents of which I can imperfectly touch. Many things observed by us I am not at liberty to mention, for the all-sufficient reason that you would not understand them and the world is not prepared to receive them.

Our first visit was to a society of literary celebrities, located in a city of marvelous beauty. For our present use we will call the place the City of Learning, and the society, the Society of the Literati. These names are not the real ones, but serve our purpose fully as well, indeed much better. The city is located on the border of a vast expanse of water of a golden hue, and this limpid stream is a vast musical organ of sounds, whose very vibrations, as its currents flow along, disturb the surrounding atmosphere, resulting in the production of harmonies in musical intonations, not only delightfully enrapturing, but far beyond the power of portrayal in human speech. We stood upon its brink, and were enchanted by its soul-piercing melody. Ever and anon the mellowed rays of the spiritual sun of our solar system would strike upon the bosom of this majestic stream, producing in their rebound such marvelous, scintillating reflections as to cause the beautiful tints of your rainbow to pale into utter insignificance in comparison. You must elaborate in your own mind these feeble touches of my pen, for I can not stop to give minute delineations, but only the idea, and you can carry it onward in your imagination without fear of overdoing the picture or exaggerating the facts.

The ladies and gentlemen composing the Society of the Literati of this one city are numbered by the many thousands, with vast numbers of co-operating branches in as many different localities. We are told that there exist still higher branches, which we were not spiritually fitted to visit and comprehend. We, as spirits from earth, lacked planetary development, but we have the promise in the infinite justice of God's eternal laws that in time, though very far distant, our earth, with its encircling spiritual spheres, will reach unto the gorgeous grandeur of Mars. Here let us pause and reflect.

March 29—Herein may be found ample food for study, inspiring elements for reflection:

First—How almighty is God, yet puny man is wondering whether there is a God.

Second—How grand and noble may all his children become.

Third—How patiently does God, through inflexible and unerring law, work out such stupendous results.

Fourth—Man while in the flesh would arrogate unto himself the attributes of a God, when in truth it requires ages of effort and progress only to disclose to him that yet he is not yet an angel. But still how grand are the possibilities before man, inviting him onward. They can not be fully conceived by the finite mind, much less described.

We saw many translucent streams, whose pellucid waters were charming to behold. There is a law appertaining to all advanced spiritual intelligences that induces the profoundest meditation, the sublimest adoration, when beholding, although only partially, the infinite variety and splendors of the creation; and I must occasionally pause in my narrative to give expression to this law of my soul.

We were next conducted to a vast building, wherein was deposited the grandest library of books, and they were simply collections on scientific subjects alone. Elsewhere were vast collections on other subjects not intimately connected with science—books as tangible and objective to us as the slate on which I am writing is to your touch and sight. Mr. Swedenborg, being naturally of a scientific turn of mind, became absorbingly interested in this department, and it was with reluctance he took his departure therefrom. He made arrangements to return to study some things to be found here and which he has not been able to find elsewhere. He is promised aid by the members of the Society of the Literati.

We then visited an assembly of representative men, and I am now about to tell you something that will surprise you, but it is nevertheless true. When I use the expression representative men I mean that each planet has representatives to every other planet in the solar system. I must reserve the next sitting for a description of the grand system of planetary diplomacy—envoys extraordinary or ministers plenipotentiary, as you would call them. The power is too nearly exhausted to enter upon the subject at this sitting. We notify you now that by these ministrations and recitals you are living many, many years in advance of this age of your planet.

April 3—In your solar system you only claim eight planets, exclusive of the Asteroids between Mars and Jupiter, but the truth is there are thirteen in number; five of them have long since passed into their spiritual orbits, and consequently are not objective to your telescopes, and this state is to be the ultimate of all planets. Every planet, including the earth, is continually undergoing change, that is to say, gradually passing from the gross to the more refined, and by a continually advancing series of geologic and progressive changes from the lower to the higher, from the crude to the more refined, from the material toward the spiritual, all will ultimately in time pass into spiritual conditions or orbits. But as this theme is scientific, and not directly in the line of or pertinent to my narrative, I will abandon it, at least for the present.

In my last I told you that each planet was favored with representatives from every other planet in our system, and it is from this system, spiritually originating, that you have derived your system of international representation. I do not mean that any spirit communicated this to the nations, but that in the early formation of nationalities and the commercial intercourse between nations, susceptible public men, by reason of their exceeding impressibility, got the inspiration from surrounding spiritual influences, and to a certain degree and extent carried it into execution in the establishment of ambassadorial relations between friendly governmental powers. But there is a marked difference between your nations and the spiritual worlds in the objects and purposes of such system. In the spiritual worlds representatives are deputed one to the other for an entirely different purpose from yours in sending ministers to England, France, Russia, etc. Your accredited agents of government abroad are simply spies to watch other countries, lest some trivial advantage may be gained against you in some minor and unimportant matter. Selfishness is the law by which they are to be governed. They are expected to be, and generally are, lorded and feasted, dined and wined, all in the high-sounding names of civilization and national urbanity. Ours are sent on an entirely different mission—to gather knowledge for the benefit of all. Our public and representative men are not engaged in learning the rules and laws of the stock market, how to manipulate it and how to create corners in the bountiful productions vouchsafed by the Infinite, nor how to secure safe investments with large and profitable margins, but to learn the laws of the planets, to the end that they may be utilized in the development and progress of their varied and numerous peoples. Through whatever other planets, farther advanced than ours—have passed, we, too, must pass, and hence by our representative spirits learning of their varied progressive experiences, they are enabled to prepare for and assist in the changes that must inevitably ensue.

I can not carry my thought further than to say in addition that our solar system, as a system in its entirety, has representatives to thousands of other solar systems revolving in space, circling around their respective central suns. You perceive that the grandeur of creative glory is looming up before us in majestic proportions, far beyond our power to comprehend and portray. We look forward with great pleasure to each succeeding meeting, when we hope to continue our narrative if conditions continue to favor us.

April 6—After feasting in the examination of the library of the Society of the Literati I felt an intense desire to learn something in regard to the religious teachings on the planet in its past, as applied to the embodied Marsians, in the curious desire to find out whether their theological and religious history bore any resemblance to ours, and if dissimilar, wherein by contrast the dissimilarity consisted. Of course, in the very nature of things, this opened up a wide field of investigation, and I can only give you points condensed and with the utmost brevity, and without any attempt at elaboration. As I have already informed you, the denizens of Mars do not use our language or mode of speech, and therefore I am compelled to transfer their thoughts into our language, and you must consider that much will be lost in the transmission.

The planet Mars, in point of time, is much older than the earth, and consequently has passed through many more changes; these successive changes or epochs have had their respective theologies, and I was utterly surprised to learn that in some respects they resembled ours—that is to say, their earlier theology—the later and truer has no resemblance whatever to ours or any that we have had in the past. The people of Mars in the dim and distant ages of the bygone have had many gods and many bibles. Their older books or bibles are now treasured as simple curiosities belonging to the infancy of the race, and the wonder now is how it was possible at any period of their history that a people could be found seemingly so hopelessly ignorant as to believe them. The same fate, my friend, awaits your Bibles, Korans, Zend-Avestas, etc. But in all their speculations in religion they were never taught to believe that their remote ancestors had fallen from an imaginary state of perfection, nor that somebody else's sufferings and death were imperatively necessary to extricate them from the peril, and to reinstate them into the loving esteem and saving grace of their creator. While they had many follies in their early history, they had none like unto our own. They never believed God to be angry and revengeful nor that he would ever destroy their own or any other world by water, fire or otherwise, nor that men were made out of dust and women from ribs, nor that fish swallowed men, preserved them in good condition in their stomachs, and delivered them subsequently and in safety upon the dry land. These silly recitals of your bible will be ridiculed and laughed at some of these coming happy days."

April 10—If you could be instantaneously transferred to the planet Mars just as you are in the form you could not live a moment of time. The intensely rarefied and etherealized atmospheres surrounding that planet would not maintain animal life such as yours. Yet the time has been when beings more crude, dense and undeveloped have lived and figured on the stage of Mars's history. The law of evolution or unceasing progression applies to all planets and in a degree of unfoldment according to the periodic duration of time of each. Hence, under the operation of this inexorable law of the creation you can readily and with quick discerning eye see the ultimate destiny of all—that is to say, the utter overcoming of the crude and unrefined by the spiritual absorption of the whole, and yet this law that lifts the lower into the higher has no limit or ending. You can therefore see in the myriad ages of future time with this law, all the while actively working, how inexpressibly refined and sublimated will become spiritual beings and spiritual essences. This constitutes a grand revelation, and presents in contemplation the grand possibilities in store for man and the fittest of all things material. While the constituent elements are the same, yet in outward manifestation the atoms composing your physical bodies, and those in the form on Mars, are quite dissimilar. The same elements that exist here, either as applied to the spiritual or material, are essentially the same as exist in the remotest realms of the creation. They only differ in presentation or outward manifestation, and in the degree of their development and progression. Here is another theme for contemplation and study, and the fact as here disclosed ought to fill us with proud satisfaction, for the inherent elements and qualities possessed by the millions of worlds, revolving in the unexplored immensity of space and their countless myriad hosts of people, are possessed by our world and our denizens, only differing in the intensity of their action and the degree of unfoldment or approximation toward maturity—ah, a maturity that never matures. While the law of progression is infinite it deals with the finite, and as the finite can only advance toward but never become infinite, so will this mighty law of progression carry us onward and onward, upward and upward through all coming time, and yet will never cease from its labors or find repose. What a mighty destiny before and for man!

April 14—In this and my next I will tell you some things that will surprise you, but they are veritably true. I am dealing with you in verities, however absurd and preposterous they may appear to the unprogressed mind. This is said, by your people, to be a remarkable age, and in many respects it is so. You are receiving some matter far in advance of the age in which you are living, but it will be properly recognized and appreciated in the years to come.

On the planet Mars jails and prison houses for the confinement and punishment of malefactors are only historic reminiscences of the past. There are now no punishments inflicted because there are no offenders to punish.

The doctrine of sacrificial atonement, with its retarding influence, was never taught to the people of that planet. They have always been taught the supreme goodness of the creator conjoined with wisdom and almighty power. God being supremely good, and supreme in the exercise of goodness, they have not for thousands of years last past entertained the slightest apprehension that any onslaught upon their peace, happiness, and future felicity, would be permitted. From this ennobling conception of God came the desire to manifest a spirit of devotion and veneration, and consequently at an earlier period of the history of Mars the worship of the people was low and groveling somewhat resembling, as I am informed, the ancient idol worship of the Egyptians and Israelites. At the present time the two worlds—the spiritual and material—of Mars are so closely allied and interblended that the spiritual forces are enabled to exercise a positively restraining influence over the conduct and actions of those still connected with the physical, so they can not, if they would, commit wrong, or perpetrate infractions upon the law of right. By reason of this high condition of development those passing out of the material form are at once intromitted into the higher conditions of the spiritual world, because they are fitted for them. All are mediums and subject absolutely to spiritual action and control. This is what your spirit world is seeking to do for you, so, if possible, to pass over and beyond some of the rough experiences of other planets, and your people do not seem to have the good sense to see it. On Mars there are no murders, arsons, robberies, forgeries, slanders, and other crimes and misdeeds, for they have progressed beyond them. Do you not perceive the sublimity of this condition? and will it not be a most glorious consummation when you shall have reached the same altitude of progress.

April 17—Another subject of inquiry engrossed my attention, namely, marriage. I became interested to know something of the history of this people on this subject, and I found it to be an exceedingly interesting one. At this period of Mars there is no such institution as marriage in the sense you regard it. It is not an exaggeration to say that a very large per cent of your marriages are brought about as the result of the most unholy motives. Passion, lust, avarice, etc., are generally the impelling influences, and seldom is witnessed a union from purely spiritual causes. It is needless to say these marriages are not only temporal, ending with the death of the body, if not sooner by an unholy judicial system of divorcement, but entail a cruel blighting curse upon the race.

The history of your own planet on the subject of marriage is but feebly understood by you. Enough however is known to induce all lovers of humanity to loathe and detest it as it has been practiced in the past. It is claimed that God created animate creatures in pairs, male and female, and that, as applied to man, he cemented a union of one man and one woman in the marriage relation, and that this occurred at the commencement of the creation in the Garden of Eden. Your conspicuous bible characters, such as Abraham, David, Solomon, and others, have not only ignored and trampled upon virtue in its simplest and purest forms, but with the hellish gluttony of the vampire feasting on blood, they debauched innocence, prostituted virtue to their unholy lust, and thereby destroyed the holiest relation of life. Their numerous wives and concubines attest this, and yet your pious Christians are waging a relentless warfare upon the Mormons of Utah and vehemently thundering against the polygamous practices of the Latter Day Saints. Shame for Christian consistency. On this subject your advanced thinkers do not discuss those eternal and enduring spiritual laws of attraction by magnetic and soul affinity upon which alone shines forth in eternal splendor the blending of soul with soul in an everlasting conjugal union. The people of Mars understand and adopt these laws, or rather harmonize and abide in them, and now while embodied their marriages are for all unending future time. As the result we discover on that planet a race of people almost perfect in their mental, moral, and physical developments, requiring only time, experience, and progression, to disclose the still more wonderful proportions of their being. The union of one man and one woman under spiritual conditions is the highest type of marriage, and constitutes the paramount and supreme intention of the deity, and is the ultimatum and consummation of the law of conjugal love—all others are fleeting, dishonoring, and only evil.

April 20—Your candidates for matrimony, first obtaining each other's consent, and the approval of parents or guardians, apply to the legally constituted authorities for a license or permit to enter the holy state, and when procured they repair to a priest or magistrate, who for a few shekels pronounces a few stereotyped phrases, followed by the solemn declaration pronouncing them man and wife, closing generally with the ludicrous and farcical command, 'whom God has joined together let no man put asunder.' Oh, what a caricature and farce. It is bad enough to declare whom the law has joined together, and so forth, but to assume with such solemn gravity that God has joined in wedlock's sacred union many of the marriage alliances which are mere caricatures of marriage, is not only blasphemy, but the very apex of nonsense, and is the widest possible departure from truth.

If it be true that God joins them together, no power, save himself could put asunder or disunite. To assert otherwise would amount to affirming that God is the author of failures. The difference between marriages that only have their basis in consent, license, and ceremony, and that marriage which God cements when two are joined by the divine laws of soul affinity and magnetic attraction—the one is of the earth earthy, the other is from the Lord through and by the operation of eternal law, and is therefore heavenly. Oh, that the children of earth might learn and conform to these subtle and glorious laws for their own good and in the interest of those to come after them.

On the planet Mars the people have no license system on any subject. While you on earth are wrangling about licensing the sale of intoxicating beverages, on Mars they have none to license. While here you are exercised over measures of taxation to raise revenue to support the government, on Mars no taxes whatever are imposed, and public affairs for the general public good are administered freely and without compensation, purely as a labor of love. The truth is that the mundane affairs of Mars are more regulated, controlled, and conducted by the spiritual powers of the planet than by those in the form. The two worlds are so intimately related to each other, and are so closely brought together, that this is not only practicable but desirable and profitable.

April 21—There is on the planet Mars a subterranean passage through it from pole to pole, which Mr. Swedenborg informs me he has thoroughly explored. There is more truth than poetry in what is known as Symmes' hole as applied to your earth. When the time comes by the settlement of your as yet vast millions of uninhabited acres, and a change takes place in northern temperature and conditions, the people of that day will discover within and through the very heart center of your earth a country nearly a third as large as the exterior surface, and by that time every thing therein will be sufficiently progressed and developed to supply the wants and invite the ambition and energies of the people of that period. But this discovery, or rather the occupation of this subterranean country, is very far off in point of time, and the human race of earth will then be quite different from what it is now. They will have so changed by the lapse of time and the law of progress as to be enabled to pass into the new country by way of the north pole with ease and safety. The north pole is the true opening, and can not be reached until the fullness of time, as I have indicated. As the area of territory of Mar's surface was about being densely covered by population, and apprehensions were being entertained for the future of the race, lo and behold, the new interior country was discovered and subsequently peopled. By the time it is crowded no more will be needed, for the planet by that time will have passed into its spiritual orbit and into the ocean of spiritual ether, where suffering can never come from lack of room. This will be the future history of your planet, and you will pass through the same experiences and reach the same ultimate. Behold how infinitely wise all things are forearranged. Just as we need by our development new limits, new appliances and new things, they are ready for our use, and are never disclosed until we are ready for and need them.

April 24—At this time those living on the planet Mars do not die or pass through the change called death as you do here. They have no diseases that cause the untimely taking off of the inhabitants. Disease has long since been banished. All of the procreating elements of disease residing in the materiality of the globe or the surrounding atmosphere have been by progressive development eliminated. And even before this had fully occurred the people had learned the laws of health and the process of neutralizing and rendering harmless the lurking germs that remained. You may perceive from this what a happy people they are. There are no untimely deaths on Mars. Children grow up to manhood and womanhood; yet there is no fixed standard of time when all die, that is, no definite and invariable period of longevity. And right here comes in a great law, now operative on Mars, that the people of earth know nothing about, for it has never been communicated before, namely, children can not die there. It was never designed that they should die here. Marriage being brought about, as before stated, by the grand law of magnetic attraction or spiritual affinity, and all diseases being banished and their producing causes annihilated, nothing but absolutely sound and perfect physical and mental organizations are imparted to offspring by their progenitors. You see at once the idea, for I must be brief—the children being perfect in health of body and mind by procreation, and there being no diseases to affect them after birth, death can not touch them, in fact can touch none before the time arrives, varying in point of longevity for the separation of spirit and body. None die before the full maturity of stature, and some live to be a very advanced age. After reaching complete development or stature, they pass out of and away from the material in point of time, according to the antecedent conditions of their varied being. Some arrive after maturity to the estate of progressive experience in the form sooner than others, and when this period arrives, whether it be at thirty, forty, fifty or a hundred years, they pass on to their ultimate and higher state of being in the spiritual spheres. It is known when each shall pass out of the form long before the event transpires, and all due preparation is accordingly made therefor. Your scientists have discovered, and rightly, too, that about every seven years the atoms and particles composing your physical organizations change and give way to new ones. But this is gradual and imperceptible. On Mars, at this period of development, the changes are much more frequent, and these successive changes determine the approach of dissolution, and instead of death in an hour or a day, it goes on perceptibly and without pain or suffering for years. Every change lessens the material composites of the body, and at each a nearer approach to the spiritual takes place, until finally the physical, by the gradual process of embodied sublimation or attenuation, passes away, and the spiritual becomes supreme. This culmination is equivalent to what you call death, except that there is no attending pain, no death struggle, and no physical body afterwards to take care of and lay away. The body, by successive changes, has seemingly vanished into nothingness and been absorbed in the atmosphere.

April 27—We have been expecting you to inquire of us how the people live on the planet Mars, what kind of architecture in the construction of their business houses, habitations, etc.; what kind of food they eat, and with what raiment are they clothed, etc.

You will have observed from what we have heretofore made known to you that the services of four classes of professional worthies have been dispensed with, simply because the people have progressed beyond their utility, namely, lawyers, doctors, preachers and politicians. Lawyers can only thrive and exist professionally in a land where conscience is not permitted to exercise its native simplicity and positive purity, and where the lower passions and propensities are largely dominant. When conscience, active, pure and simple, is allowed to manifest its functions in perfect unrestraint, and to act as the governing power in the regulation of human conduct, the presence and office of the barrister are no longer of use. Lawyers flourish as a general proposition on strife and contention, bad faith and unfair dealing; and when these shall happily end, like poor cashiered Cassio, their occupation will be gone. The doctors grow opulent by medication, because of the ignorance of the people with reference to the true laws of marriage, proper antenatal conditions, neglect of proper hygiene, and ignorance as to overcoming or rendering harmless the deleterious conditions, both atmospheric and from the undeveloped state of inherent nature. But when, by progressing beyond their harmful influences, or by enlightenment and healing gifts, the people shall obtain a complete mastery over them, disease shall be banished, then the avocation of the physician ends, and he will have to seek a livelihood in other pursuits.

The preacher lives in comfortable indolence because of the ignorance and superstition of the people. His office is one of hypocrisy and fraud. Hypocrisy, because if he is not a fool, he knows his teachings are not true, and of fraud, because by dissembling he extorts from his parishoners a dishonorable subsistence. When the people grow sufficiently wise they will be taught by the denizens of the spirit world truth and righteousness. Then the mission or office of the sacerdotal gentlemen will be closed, and they can seek employment in the many more honorable occupations. The politician, cunning and subtle, swims along smoothly upon the rolling current of the credulity of the people and his own duplicity. He prospers because you have not as yet grown into full political manhood, and he succeeds in hoodwinking you with the belief that his heart is overflowing with patriotism and anxious solicitude for the public weal. But I must leave this class—the politicians—to the tender mercies of several gentlemen who are waiting the opportunity to contribute their part to your enterprise.

April 28—The coarse food necessary for you in order to keep up the crude materiality of which your physical make-up is composed, is not needed by the denizens of Mars. In the composition of your physical bodies is a representative of all the material elements in nature—iron, calcium, wood, earth, etc.—and it is easily demonstrated by microscopic inspection and chemical analysis, that in every drop of blood in the human system all these varied and numerous elements are represented. Hence man may be safely considered a microcosm, or nature in her vast domain, reflected in miniature. But you still exist in the realm of the crude, and yet you are vastly more refined than in the ages past, and forward, onward, and upward is the line of march marked out for you by the infinitely wise director of all things. On the planet Mars no animal food is used, because among other reasons the physical properties of the body do not require the elements of animal flesh to replace nature's wastes. Thousands of former species of animals have become extinct, swallowed up in the ever-surging maelstrom of progression or absorbed in the higher forms. Vegetation in the planet Mars is quite different, both in expression or appearance, and constituent composition from the vegetation of your planet. Here the aroma residing in the vegetable and escaping therefrom, is largely absorbed and neutralized by the grossness of the vegetable itself, while on Mars the grossness has become so diminished that to the senses the aroma has almost become tangibly objective, and this aroma is food strengthening and invigorating, is nearly sufficient of itself to support existence in the form without the assistance of the more substantial fibers of the parent vegetable. Yet in a certain prepared form the substantial material is used. The time is not very far distant, as I am assured, when the people there will subsist on aromatic emanations from material productions, aided by magnetic, electric, and other atmospheric properties used simply by inhalation. In the water you use are to be found teeming millions of living and moving animalcules. They are enabled to live on the elements of the water in its present gross state, but on the planet Mars the water has been dispossessed of its life germinating and life sustaining properties to aquatic productions, and has thus progressed with all other things and beings. No life or form of life is now brought into being there, but such higher types as are fitted to pass with the planet into spiritual conditions; and the water being so purified by nature's refining processes is as different from your ordinary water as clear, sparkling sprays projected from your fountains and dancing in the sunbeams are to the murky waters of your rivulets immediately after a violent rain-storm. I will resume this subject in my next.

May 1—On Mars they have learned how to produce from the soil itself any vegetable that naturally grows therefrom. In the soil itself reside all the constituent elements of all vegetation in their infinite variety. You may thoughtlessly answer, that in order to produce any species of vegetation used for table consumption, the seed or germ must first be sown in the soil beneath the surface, but you forget that this process is but the result of civilization and art, and that originally, that is before you learned how to obtain and use seed, the products sprang of themselves and apparently spontaneously from the earth. Whence did they come? and whence were their germinating and generating powers obtained? Think a little deeply on the subject, and you will be led irresistibly to the correct conclusion that in the soil exists all the requisite elements in the production of vegetation by growth. The people of Mars have acquired the knowledge which enables them to produce out of the soil, abstractly considered, all the essential qualities of the vegetable without waiting for the tedious process of growth. This process is purely chemical, and everybody there understands it. Hence you see they do not have to buy vegetables, for all can have their essential qualities for food without cost to the consumer. Long since the ownership of the soil by individuals was abandoned for the general common good, and on this subject the primitive condition of affairs in your planet prevails universally on Mars—that is to say everybody owns realty, one just as much as another. This is pure unadulterated agrarianism in its highest and most perfect form.

It is often asked in your intercourse with the world of spirits: What are the employments of spirits? what are they about? what do they do? etc. It is pertinent to inquire, What are the employments of the people of Mars still embodied? What do they do since we have discovered that they do not now toil for the acquisition of riches, because they have no possible use for them; no taxes to pay, no governmental machinery to support, no lawyers to annoy, no preachers to vex, torture, and maintain, no doctors to nauseate with their drugs, no politicians to hoodwink the people and feed at the public crib, no grocery bills to look after and liquidate, etc. Before we answer these and many other important queries, we shall see what the people do for raiment with which to clothe themselves, and what they do for shelter, if, indeed, shelter is necessary. If we shall discover that these are free gifts from the father, then the employments of the embodied Marsians becomes a question of very interesting and pressing importance.

May 4—I suspect that you already anticipate the tenor of what we have to tell you in regard to the clothing of the people of Mars, what texture, how derived, etc. Your keen perceptions and astute comprehension enables you to see at a glance that if this law of progression, as applied to the material, whereby the lowest forms are reached and operated upon, lifting with its strong arms into higher and still higher conditions, be true, it must be true and in regard to all material things—the soil, rock, wood, water, etc., animal and vegetable life, and as we shall have occasion to show further on, to the mundane atmosphere surrounding the planet. All things progress and advance in like and equal ratio, leaving nothing behind or unaffected by the law. This advancing march of matter from the crude and gross into the more refined and sublimated is seemingly slow, but nevertheless sure and unerringly, indiscriminate, and precise. Therefore the raiment worn by the denizens of Mars has reached the same altitude of refinement as all other material things.

The seasons, once resembling yours, spring, summer, autumn, and winter, have nearly merged, that is to say, have nearly blended into one perpetual season of summer loveliness. The austerity of winter, with its stormy blasts and cold, piercing wind waves has long since ceased to be; no frosts to nip and blight the fruits and flowers; no chilling autumns, with withering leaf, to inspire with melancholy and sadness. What will surprise you in this connection is, that, while the cold temperature has wrought its work in the development of the past, and is only known to have once existed by historic relation, the intense heat of summer has also disappeared. When you have severely cold winters, almost unendurable even in your temperate zones, your wise philosophers theorize that your ultimate destiny is to freeze out; that the icebergs and ice glaziers of the north are ultimately either to roll over the now fair portions of the earth, destroying all things animate, or that their freezing breath will sweep over the globe involving in death all the fair and lovely forms of nature's productions, including godlike man, the apex and crowning glory of creation. But lo! when the earth straightens up on her axis and the cold waves retreat and sink away in their northern hiding place, and the genial and vernal season with its pleasant temperature returns, these same philosophers take a breathing spell, rest awhile, and conclude that it has not been so very cold after all; and when the summer comes, if it happens to be unusual in the intensity of its heat, and the solar rays seem to almost melt into molten ruin all things, and to scorch the forest leaves and wilt the waving harvests, these same philosophical wiseacres change tactics, reverse their position, and with one heroic bound jump to a directly opposite conclusion, namely: that we are all destined ultimately to burn up and become annihilated in a general conflagration by solar heat igniting the combustible material of the planet and its surrounding atmosphere. Oh, how impotent in philosophy! A simple and humble inquiry settles the question. Why destroy this fair earth, daily and hourly becoming still fairer? Does God do any thing without an all wise and beneficent purpose? Is it possible for Him to do a silly, foolish thing? He would certainly not destroy the earth unless there was thereby some noble and beneficent purpose to subserve. What grand purpose, good and wise, can be accomplished by ending the existence of a planet that has as yet scarcely begun to live? To assume that He will do such a thing, is to assume that He has become disappointed and disgusted with his own creation, which annuls His wisdom and foresight, or that He delights in folly, making a world and then destroying it because He can, or for any other silly and insufficient reason. To thus assume is to dishonor Him as a God, and to invest Him with the attributes of a devil.

    Wonderful changes do occur marking epochs, or cycles, in the history of all planets. Where you live to-day, thousands upon thousands of years ago another race of human beings lived, attaining a certain degree of development in science and art, but upon the fulfillment of their mission they passed away from the face of the earth. Where you now live was once swept over by old ocean, and where the deep waters and angry billows of the Atlantic now roll and revel once lived a race of people called the Atlantians, but their land with its embellishments of art and progressive development became submerged by the changes of the mighty waters, and now lies buried beneath its rolling deep and lashing waves. But observe in all this that the globe goes on, and succeeding developments of man and material things come forth far in advance of the former order of things. What, if in the womb of time it is reserved for Atlantis to arise from her watery entombment and to flourish again with renewed and increased grandeur, involving the submersion of other portions of the earth's surface, including your own? This would not be death to any portion of the planet in any high and exalted sense, but a progressive change, a revivifying of life, a quickening and impulsion of being in the grand advancing march of development and sublimation. As we write, the theme expands and enlarges, and as the power begins to wane we find we have not discoursed minutely on the subject of raiment, and beg your indulgence for a resume of the subject in our next.

May 5—There being, at this stage of development on Mars, no winter with its concomitants of winds and storm, snow and ice, you have no difficulty in apprehending that very light material only is needed to protect and render comfortable the persons of the people. Material of the texture of your lightest flannel underwear would be oppressively and uncomfortably warm, and indeed insufferable. Thin and quite gauzy robes composed of finely attenuated and exquisitely refined material constitute their apparel. I have told you hitherto that of the animal kingdom only the fittest have survived the marvelous successive changes in the infinite series of progressive advancements. Among those now living with the ability of propagation is an animal species somewhat resembling your sheep, but so exceedingly refined as to be remarkably striking in contrast. Of course, and in the very nature of things, the fleecy wool, or, rather velvety down, that grows upon this noble animal, so distinguished for innocence, æsthetic tastes in food and refinement in habits of life, is eminently suited for purposes of habilament, and accordingly is thus utilized. They are propagated in unlimited numbers, live to an advanced age, are the common property of all the people, and have within themselves the qualities of eternal being.

The forest and other trees, shrubs and flowers, have advanced under the same law of progress. Very many species of the olden time disappearing—the fittest only having survived. Among those now extant on the planet, is a peculiar and quite extensively cultivated species, from which is produced a fabric resembling somewhat your cotton production, with the same difference in refinement of texture as exists between your wool and that developed on Mars as herein stated. This is utilized for raiment also. Besides the people there have mastered the law that spirits employ in the materialization of garments at your materializing seances, only much finer, and out of the ambient atmosphere, filled as it is with sublimated atoms and emanations, they are enabled to collect and magnetize into solidified form appropriate garments for their use and comfort. When thus magnetized into objective and tangible being it partakes of and assumes a varied hue and color, according to the progressed and advanced state of the person using the garments. In other words the magnetic aura and spiritual emanations proceeding from the individual infiltrates and becomes interwoven in the delicate fibers of the new garment extracted and brought into being from the viewless air, imparting hue and coloration presenting different appearances, whereby the grade or degree of advancement of the individual wearer is made known and determined. Here you inquire of the spirits to know what sphere you are fitted to enter in the spirit world, there they know by this means in advance of leaving the body. Your spirits in imparting light and knowledge to you concerning their state, tell you that a spirit and its proper sphere are known by the peculiar aura, or surroundings and clothing of the individual spirit, and this is true to the letter. But on Mars this law of spirit designation that belongs to the spiritual spheres of your planet, reaches out and reveals itself in the persons of the people of Mars before they have actually entered upon the spiritual journey of life in the spiritual spheres.

Now the additional fact is disclosed to you that by reason of this mode of obtaining raiment the avocation of the merchant is of slender dimensions, and the manufacturer's art and pursuit, except as known and practiced by all alike, are now unknown on the planet Mars.

In our next we will discourse on buildings, habitations, etc. We had hoped to reach this part of the subject in this communication, but as we advance the themes and subjects broaden and expand, and we sincerely regret that the power by this process—independent slate writing—although the purest of all, will not last us at one sitting sufficiently to fully elaborate our thoughts and descriptive delineations on a given subject. It has this advantage, however, it comes directly from the materialized fingers of the spirit without the direct use of the brain of another in transmission. Adieu until our next.

May 8—The same reasons assigned in our last, why very light garments only were needed for the bodily comfort and happiness of the people of Mars apply with equal propriety, force, and truth, to the subject of their habitations.

Your rains are produced by vapors, mists, and emanations from your oceans, rivers, lakes, etc., which by virtue of solar attraction or a reversal of the law of gravitation the vapors, mists, etc., are drawn upward in space until a certain density is reached, differing in altitudes of height, when they become congealed by the force of the cold attenuated atmosphere there into small particles called rain drops, and these are carried along by the undercurrents of uncongealed clouds until a certain electro-magnetic condition is reached, when the clouds begin to empty and rid themselves of their burdened contents.

Now we have informed you of the progress the water of Mars has made in being dispossessed of its gross and weighty elements; hence there are none of these to ascend and to commingle in the formation of rain drops; hence none but the purer and refined elements of the water are exhaled and drawn upward, and consequently none but the pure and refined descend. These are in themselves comparatively light and of greatly diminished gravity, and therefore mild and pleasant in their effect. Especially does this become true as a resulting necessity, from the fact that there are no fierce winds or storms or cold temperature in the surrounding atmospheric belts or zones. The rains on Mars are more like your gentle dews of early autumn than your rains and showers. You at once take in the situation from this and preceding statements of facts that crude material structures are not necessary, even if the material for their construction could be found, and we have seen that such is not the case, for all things, including the material in detail out of which edifices are constructed, have progressed beyond and above their crude grossness.

In some portions of Mars no structures are used at all, owing to the mildness of the climate and the total absence of inclemency in the slightest degree. In other portions the beautifully developed trees, and especially those that spread out their branches near the surface of the soil, are ample for the purposes of shelter. Still in others they have a sort of building which is a grand pavilion, embracing a vast area of territory, thousands of miles in extent, under the same roof or cover, which during certain periods of the year and day become luminous and transparent. The temples and gorgeous structures, cities, and magnificent edifices have been transferred in spiritual essence to the spiritual spheres, and have ceased to be as material entities, so when the planet passes into the spiritual condition outright and in toto, all that Mars could ever boast of in architectural grandeur and excellence is preserved and perpetuated with additional luster and beauty from the finishing spiritual touches by the Infinite Master Builder. And now you perceive that other questions come up right here and require recognition and treatment. Among them these: Do the people on Mars sleep? If so, how often and how much?

May 11—Why is it that you require repose in sleep? In the infinitely wise arrangement of all things there are amply satisfactory reasons for every demand, every requirement, every manifestation, and therefore there are reasons why sleep is induced and is an imperative necessity in your present and past states of existence.

When rest in sleep is long deferred from nervous derangements or other causes, your physicians administer narcotics to induce it, for they well know, as you all do, that sleep is necessary after intervals of wakefulness in order to protract your being in the form, and why?

You have voluntary and involuntary functions or organs; the voluntary only, the involuntary never, can be suspended for certain periods of time. Your respiration and blood circulation are involuntary, and as long as you remain embodied in flesh will continue to perform their appropriate functions, whether you wake or sleep, for they are not subject to or influenced by the will. And it is by the unconscious operation of these that your voluntary functions when suspended in sleep are replenished and reinvigorated. You are, as at present constituted, made up corporally of gross material, which becomes wearied and exhausted by the active exercise or operation of the voluntary functions, and the nerve force will expend itself unless periodically reimbursed and replenished, and restored to its normal condition by the intervention and recuperative power of sleep. When in the ages to come your people lose this grossness in their material composition, your inclination to sleep and the necessity for it will abate and become lessened correspondingly to your successive stages of advancement in progressive development.

Thus is revealed to you the fact that on Mars, at this time, the inhabitants have but very little need of sleep. They sleep, but in a modified sense as to periods, duration and manner. They rest when fatigued, and for brief periods pass into a state of languor or stupidity, to some extent analogous to your sleeping state, which is never required oftener than once a week, and then only for a few hours.

"Your spirit friends will tell you that they never sleep, but rest, and ever keep in mind that the people of Mars are closely approximating the spiritual. Then, again, on Mars they do not have night as you do, and consequently not the same nocturnal influences to suggest and invite sleep. This suggests another subject germane to our line of thought. In nature you find always two extremes, that seem to stand in antipodal relations to each other. Let us give a few instances in illustration: You have day and night, cold and heat, male and female, fire and water, good and evil, etc. Some of these seem to be at fierce war with each other, and yet what a delusion! This seeming antagonism is but the working of a law that shall eventuate in the production of the completest harmony. Undeveloped people, ignorant of the jewel-crowned truths, as yet concealed from them in the grand arcana of nature and the progressive sciences, laugh and sneer at the idea of marriages in spirit life, when the unvarnished truth is that man, considered in his independent and separate sexual relation, is but a half man, and can not become rounded out into fully developed manhood until consociated in conjunctive union with the opposite sex—not indeed and truly until the man and woman become twain, one flesh, or, in better phraseology, spiritually unitized.

The day and night will continue until finally and by gradual processes the night is banished, and vanishes in the splendor of a continuously refulgent and sunlit atmosphere. On Mars this condition is almost reached, and the night there resembles the shadings thrown over the earth when a cloud passes over the face of your moon at hightide, and ultimately even this shall be no more, for in the spiritual spheres of Mars, as in your exalted ones, there are no shadows to obscure or mar the radiant light of the spiritual sun, and Mars itself is fast approaching this sublime condition. We must withhold what we have to say in regard to the seeming strife between good and evil for our next.

May 12—The people of christendom have had it rung in their ears for nearly two thousand years that man is essentially bad, unutterably wicked, unspeakably depraved, and, worst of all, this horrid state comes to him, not of his own creating, but by inevitable and unavoidable inheritance. In our ignorance and credulity how we have wept over the weakness and folly of our first parents in yielding to the flattery and persuasive eloquence of the cruel serpent in the pure and primitive bowers of Eden. Our tears have flown and flown, with no gentle, soothing hand to touch our eyes and bid them cease; no voice panoplied with authority to speak to; no words of hope and cheer. We have been told in answer to our anxious entreaties for blissful hope and loving counsel that there is a superabundance of evil in us, and a trifling, insignificant quantity of good, and that nothing short of a miracle of regeneration can save us from unutterable and unending misery in the life to come; that without this miraculous interposition of divine grace, the little good that is in us will be swallowed up and devoured by the appalling evil of our sinfully inherited natures. Oh, man, how you degrade your true nobility, your godlike and divine nobility, by bowing the knee to this hideous monster of falsehood, and by kneeling at this unholy shrine. In direct opposition to this abominable and degrading doctrine stands the truth in its pristine and noble beauty.

According to this Christian doctrine we behold in man a combination of good and evil, and in the struggle for the mastery the evil is to be mightier than the good. The good emanating from and partaking of the majestic excellence of the eternal, infinite God must, alas, succumb to and be overthrown by evil, its unholy rival. Can man conceive of a scheme more degrading and heartless, and more completely dishonoring to God and his infinite perfections of wisdom, goodness and power—a doctrine more utterly subversive of moral goodness, deific excellence, and that more completely wrecks the moral government of God and dumps into one common funeral heap the hopes and happiness of the human race. No, no, this is not true; it is false, false, basely false.

What is the true theory of good and evil? Man, oh, man, hearken to the voice of truth, and be wooed and won by its gentle entreaties. Let the scales of ignorance and superstition fall from your eyes. Look upward for truth, and be baptized in its beauteous light, and cleansed in its pure and holy waters. Evil is the assemblage of elements in the concrete, if I may be permitted so to speak, and is simply undeveloped good, or good in a lesser degree. Evil is evanescent and transitory, good is permanent and eternally enduring. The fittest of all things in the grand scheme of progression only survive, while all else is doomed to perish. The good and the true are as enduring and everlasting as the eternal God himself, while the evil and the false are fleeting, unenduring, and carry within themselves the insatiate and unappeasable elements of ultimate annihilation. Be assured of this, for no truth in God's illimitable universe has been more firmly established on a more indestructible foundation. Good day.

May 15—Astronomers will tell you that in their observations through the telescope the planet Mars presents a red brilliancy not observably characteristic of the other planets in your solar system, which they are unable to account for. Considering the vastness of the subject, the immense distance in space where the scintillating orbs are chanting their silent songs of praise to God, the difficulties in the way of observation, etc., the discoveries in the domain of astronomy have been fully as remarkable, important, and satisfactory, as in any other field of scientific investigation. But still only a very little compared with the immensity of the subject has been disclosed and some of that mixed and interlarded with error. Astronomy will become the greatest of all sciences when by new apparatus and new appliances the spiritual spheres belonging to the various planets shall have been discovered. This success will be achieved in the coming time. On Mars the people have mastered this problem, and I was surprised to learn that they knew all about our spiritual spheres from their far distant standpoint of observation, and that they knew minutely all the characteristic and inherent qualities of your planetary atmosphere. They have long since invented instruments by which they are enabled to photograph in minute detail and perfect fidelity of representation every material object on the earth. And you will be surprised when I tell you that I inspected Stockholm, London, Paris, New York, your own queen city, Cincinnati, etc., in a more perfect form of presentation than your artists can reproduce on canvas with pencil and brush, and at the same time I was standing in spirit in the immeasurable immensity of space on the planet Mars. I can not give you even in outline, much less in detail, the modus operandi of this achievement, and will only say that the rays of light in reflective power will yet dawn upon your scientists and philosophers as the agent of discoveries and accomplishments not now even dreamed of by the people of earth. I want to add right here a prophetic statement, which you may carefully note, that the time is not so very far distant when your inspired inventors will devise and construct an instrument that will disclose to the human material eye, to the astonishment of the world, your own spirit land; for let it be well understood that your spirit world has a real, tangible, objective existence, that will yet yield its rich treasures in scientific revealments for the enlightenment and progress of your race. In very truth the spirit world is the only real and permanent one, constructed by the infinite master builder for all eternal time, while your physical and material, except their spiritual essences, are but the shadows and temporary projections from the spiritual. Logically and metaphysically speaking, the spirit world is the pre-eminent cause of your world, the mere transitory effect. This being true, your keen sense hastens you at once to the conclusion, founded in reason and truth, that an effect can not be greater or more enduring than the cause that produced it, but must of necessity and in the very nature of things be infinitely less.

May 18—A people so pre-eminently advanced in all that appertains to the sublimation of their being, and all that surrounds them, and in which they come in contact, must necessarily be exceedingly refined and æsthetic in their mannerisms, habits of life, intercourse with each other, and in their vocations and employments. In the very nature of things it could not be otherwise. From what has been heretofore said relating to the highly favored and inestimably progressed denizens of Mars, it is not difficult to see that their pursuits must necessarily and almost entirely relate to the realm of the intellectual and spiritual, as they have passed beyond the requirements and demands of that which pertains to the material phase of existence. Physical wants require physical exertion to supply them. Material requirements necessitate attention to and labor in the domain of the material, and this, for obvious reasons, that need not be stated or discussed. It may be prudent, however, to premise that when the physical constitution requires substantially gross materials to keep up and maintain the corporealities of our nature, we must look to the productions of the farm and the fruitage of the forest, and also to animal food, which are always in quality and degree in exact correspondence to our status or state of progression. But when we lose the constituent elements of corporeal being that belong to the lower strata of the constitution of things, we require something more refined and sublimated, and lo, always it is at hand to meet the exigency, for let it ever be borne in mind that the law that is incessantly and without intermission working away in solving the great problem of life and being, moving upward from the lower to the higher, is not confined in its operations to only form or species of being, but applies to and operates upon all, whether rational or irrational, animate or inanimate, and pushes all forward and upward with perfect and precise equability and in exact and equally proportional degree, none advancing more rapidly than the rest and none lagging behind. Thus, you perceive the infinite order and the beautiful symmetry of the great law of evolution and progression. Herein is necessitated varied changes in the value and character of vocation and employments, suited to the continued mutations of things in the endless series of progressive changes.

At one period in the history of Mars the art of photography was discovered. Of course it attracted great attention and challenged admiration. It was regarded not only as wonderful but marvelous. The discoverer was almost deified, for he was thought to be endowed with something of the divine nature not discoverable in others, until the art advanced step by step, improvement on improvement, when the divinity with which the discoverer had been invested by the admiring multitudes dwindled into insignificance, and the very sensible conclusion reached that he was merely highly gifted and spiritually inspired, but altogether human still. Compare the primitive system of photography, limited as it was, to objects of immediate presence to that now existing, whereby worlds and systems of worlds are made tributary to its discoveries and achievements. Now, instead of the wonders of the art inspiring hero worship of the men engaged in its studies and who produce the wondrous results, a feeling of awe and veneration for the continually increasing wonders of the creation is inspired. The admiration is justly transferred from man to the creator and the stupendous majesty of his laws and works. On Mars photography is now and has been for a long time a favorite and delightful employment pursued by the many, for all have the advantages of it. Therefore the study, not only of their own world, but numerous others, constitutes a pleasant, instructive, and intellectually remunerative employment. Nor is this confined and limited to material worlds, but reaches out and embraces the spiritual spheres of each.

Again, take the science of chemistry. It once only dealt with material solids, but now on Mars it has reached a higher plane or sphere, and the sublimated substances, still possessed of modified degrees of matter, likewise atmospheric and spiritual substances, come within the purview and yield obedience to its powerful processes of analysis. This is still and ever will be an instructive and profitable field for those aspiring minds of the Marsians bent on the acquisition of knowledge and the understanding of the infinitely varied and universal laws by which all nature and the universe are governed and controlled.

May 22—On Mars the people are divided up into a very great many societies. The membership of these societies is not a matter of choice and volition. Here you have degrees of social society, and you say there are three grades—the lower, middle and upper. This is so in the deceptive seeming, but in fact you have many more, but you do not understand the subtle laws governing in their formation and diversity. You also have secret societies, into which you require the consent of a certain number to gain admission, while at the same time a certain other number may object. Certain arbitrary votes in number control the question of application, and by them your admission or rejection is determined. In your social society quite a different rule or policy prevails. In a certain grade or stratum true merit and worth are not considered of any moment, but wealth and pecuniary par excellence constitute the law of attraction. In other words, and what ought to burn your cheeks with shame, it matters not how morally depraved or utterly abandoned to all real intrinsic worth of manhood or womanhood, a large supply of the world's fleeting possessions constitutes the real standard of respectability, and the sure passport into the higher walks of social life. On Mars they have long since passed beyond and above this purely human, unspiritual and unholy rule. There they are known and estimated as they really are, for they can not disguise their moral and spiritual status; it is read in the look, the walk, the thought-words, and most potently in the aura emitted, permeating and coloring the very garments worn, thereby disclosing by shades of color the moral, mental and spiritual degree of advancement. You have an old adage, which contains a very great truth, namely: 'Birds of a feather will flock together,' 'like draws like.' Under the operation of an immutable law of attraction and repulsion the societies of Mars are formed, and this law, so utterly disregarded by embodied man on the earth, applies to and is operative in the spiritual spheres of all the innumerable worlds of the vast, illimitable universe of God. And this law of attraction and repulsion is indiscriminate and recognizes no distinction on account of wealth, social standing or prominence among men. It deals with spiritual laws and spiritual truths and spiritual things. There being different societies on Mars, formed and governed by this great and inexorable law of selection or attraction and repulsion, you see readily that their employments must of necessity and in some regards be quite different.

May 29—We have endeavored to keep before you, at the risk of being censured for occasional reiteration and repetition, the great primary and fundamental fact that all things under the divine arrangement advance in the ascending scale of infinite and unending progression by regular and gradual series, and in equal ratio; but you must note an important fact in this connection, namely, that all do not at the same time reach the same degree of unfoldment—some a little in advance of others, and so on. The question necessarily arises, why is this so? We only desire to say in answer at this time that all do not start out on their career of animate being at precisely the same time or under the same conditions, nor with the same or equal antenatal advantages. This carries us back behind our mere entrance into physical life, through and by the laws of human physical procreation, into a domain as yet unexplored, except feebly, by mortal man. It seems to me if men could only perceive and understand the grand sublimity and variety of their antecedent being, they would no longer be blinded to the future greatness and glory in store for them. This subject, if you ever enter upon it, you will find prolific of vast knowledge, immense and perfectly astounding revelations. But the time has not yet arrived for them. The people on Mars, like your own, not starting out on life's eventful and momentous journey with the same or equal advantages, have necessarily attained unto different degrees of progressive unfoldment, and by reason of this are their different and somewhat differing societies formed. In the same circle, order or stratum of society on earth, the good, the bad and the indifferent associate and seem to harmoniously blend and assimilate. But this is not true in fact. The degree of perfection attained in moral and spiritual excellence does not govern in their formation, and they are therefore incongruous, unsatisfactory and transitory. On Mars two unequals in progression can not harmonize, for the law rebels, interposes insurmountable barriers, and will not allow it. Those only are associated who harmonize and resemble each other, not in the accumulations of wealth, not in stature, not in facial expressions or outward physical conformation, but those who are drawn together by a sort of soul kinship, of absolute union of soul feeling, sympathetic inclinations and aspirations, having for their basis, as of prime and first importance, an equal degree of spiritual unfoldment. Thus divided and separated, there are very many different societies or orders, each differing in development, inclinations and aspirations, they inevitably have dissimilar pursuits and employments, suited to tastes, wants and abilities, but all conspiring for the general good of all.

June 1—The people of Mars are not so large in stature as on your earth, nor are they as large as at former periods of their history. The process of progression in casting off the gross, and also by affecting the laws of propagation, has materially reduced the present inhabitants in their physical proportions. Their feet, except in the lower order, are either not shod at all, or are covered by a very light and refined material substance. The nearer the spiritual the people become the less they are affected by grosser atmospheric elements, and this is directly the opposite of your experience. Here the coarser the material make-up the better can the severer conditions of your temperature be borne, and the reason is plain.

Here some are progressed, physically speaking, in advance of the progress of the elements, and therefore they are detrimentally affected and influenced by them, whereas on Mars a regular advance in development has been reached, and all things now smoothly and evenly pass under the operations of the law. After awhile the same law will commence to thus orderly and regularly operate with you when this difficulty will be happily overcome. The grandest achievement made by progression on Mars has produced the greatest result in the formation of the heads of the people. Phrenology here on earth is but feebly and imperfectly understood, although there is in it a grand and most salutary scientific truth. Here, however, as yet, you have the angular and uneven formation of the cranium, with its attendant angularity of temperament and disposition. On Mars the heads are so exquisitely formed and so harmonious in the external, and so perfectly symmetrical, that you observe and note it at first glance, and following this high and beautiful development is discovered a degree of wisdom and learning perfectly astonishing to a visitor from a foreign, though neighboring planet. The hair on these magnificent heads is of a fiber and texture resembling your finest silk, and from under a beautifully arched brow you behold a mild yet brilliant eye, beaming with intelligence and affection, and they can convey thoughts and ideas without the use of words or the intervention of audible sound.

June 5—Hundreds, yea, thousands of years ago, the development of mind on the planet Mars was extraordinary, and you can conceive what it must be now. Many causes, of course, conspired and aided in bringing about this result. The natural process of development would have ultimately accomplished it unassisted by other agencies, but a wise and humane governmental system was adopted, originating in the spirit world, which constituted a complete innovation upon and revolution in previous systems, and which gave a marked impetus to the growth and advancement of mind, and which produced also a wonderful improvement in the physical constitutions of succeeding generations. That system consisted of a legislative policy of the controlling government, rigidly and unexceptionally enforced, which provided that all children born into physical life should be given up and relinquished to the control and direction of the government, and by the government reared, educated, and prepared for the duties and requirements of life. Elaborate buildings, elaborately and artistically embellished and beautified were constructed at proper and convenient locations, where at a certain period of gestation, very early indeed, the expectant mother was taken and kept until a certain and proper time after parturition, when the mother was discharged and restored to freedom, and the new-born babe was taken charge of, raised and maintained by the fostering care of the government. Between the period of conception and parturition, the mother was continually kept under the most elevating influences, both of body and mind. Her soul was kept enraptured by the ennobling influences of music, and such music, of which you as yet have no conception. This produced in the mother the desired condition of harmony, which had a corresponding effect upon the little one concealed from mortal view. Twice or thrice a week lecturers, under the pay and patronage of the government, visited these asylums and discoursed to the inmates on scientific, literary, and moral subjects.

June 8—These discourses were not only designed but efficacious in directing the minds and hearts of the auditors into the most elevating and progressively intellectual channels, and left their inevitable and unfailing impress upon the forthcoming offspring. In addition works of art, rare paintings, and exhibitions of sculpture were at certain times presented for inspection, study, and reflection, inspiring noble thoughts of the sublime and beautiful. Artists of superior attainments and national renown occasionally visited these places and gave exhibitions of their skill in transferring to canvas, in an impromptu manner, their loftiest conceptions of the beautiful in landscapes, scenes, etc., which were of the rarest beauty of design. Books treating of the noblest subjects were placed within ready reach and convenient access, and the inmates read them with avidity and delight. They understood that they were thus preparing the new generations, as yet unushered into life, to take their places, and that their success largely depended on the assiduity with which they availed themselves of their opportunities. The government, as before stated, took charge of the young and trained and educated them in art, music, and the sciences, and the result was soon manifest in producing a race of intellectual giants, and distinguished for their ability in the arts and sciences, and the benevolence or their religious natures. And to-day you can not find a man or woman of adult age who is not perfectly versed in all the higher branches of learning, and eminently proficient in music. If a thousand of them could be bodily transferred to America, and with her exceptional advantages, and live, they would soon, by the sheer force of intellect, rule this world, and lift it morally and intellectually upon a plane that would dazzle you to behold. And yet, my dear friend, it is laid up in the womb of time that you of earth shall reach this sublime height.

The denizens of earth may wonder at and disbelieve these relations, but nevertheless they are as true as that the eternal God is truth. They point to the destiny in store for the future inhabitants of earth, and intimate to poor disheartened mortals the certainty and greatness of the future, in which they are to figure in no mean way nor act no inconsequential part.

July 10—On Mars the doctrine of discrimination on the score of sex was never taught, but the equality of the sexes has always been recognized. This indiscrimination has always been operative in employments and in the choosing of persons to fill official station at a period of their history when officers were paid out of the public exchequer for their services. Of course, at this time when office is administered without compensation the rule remains undisturbed. Your troubles, that is, many of them, in the present and past have arisen either from a misunderstanding of the truth or a misapplication of it and its requirements. Can it be rationally maintained that truth and justice require a discrimination to be made adverse to the female? If so, there must be ample reasons for it, and what are they? We are told that, comparatively speaking, woman is the weaker. Is this true? and if so, pray tell wherein? You answer physically, and thus you would establish her status in all other regards, by the rule of mere brute force, powers of endurance, and physical capabilities. Do you not know that the ox and the horse, for precisely the same reason, can largely discount you? Do you not realize that by this argument you are appealing to the lowest element of your nature, that which only distinguishes you as connected with matter, and which as we have already seen, is transitory and fleeting? Pray lift the subject upon a higher and nobler plane and then let us have your arguments and reasoning. Is man superior to woman morally? Now, if you are honest, you must blush. In morals, man superior to woman! We all know this is not true. And do morals count for naught in the scale of being? In what pertains to the finer sensibilities and spiritual pureties is woman inferior? If not, are these of no moment compared with mere physical brute force? Do women survive death as men do; if so, which will be of greatest value in the beautiful hereafter—brute force and physical prowess, which only have existence in the lower realms of the spiritual world, or those finer spiritual qualities possessed by woman in a much higher degree than by man as they manifest in embodied life, and which belong to the higher spiritual sphere of being in the other life?

Beware, oh man, how you treat angelic woman, for the future will teach you many lessons, brought about by your arbitrary and utterly indefensible assumptions and arrogations, among which will be classed your illiberal and unjust treatment of woman. She is your equal, and your great weakness is in withholding it from her.

July 13—In giving briefly and very imperfectly a sketch of what I saw and learned on the planet Mars I have been compelled necessarily to omit many things, among other reasons, because they would not only be not believed, but in many instances incite unfavorable comments, if not absolute ridicule. I am not unconscious of the fact that many things contained in the foregoing narrative, although literally true, will meet with unfavorable criticism, but I have not been writing to please or to avoid censure, but to deliver the truth, much of which I am aware is far in advance of the age in which you now live on the planet earth. But it has been thought that a little work of this kind would be kindly received and amiably treated by at least progressed minds—those who had inspirationally and intuitively drank at the fountain of spiritual wisdom and spiritual things; and, as to others, it was hoped it might cause them to think it possible, if not probable, that man is something more than a mere fleeting bauble, a mere creature of a moment.

To awaken in man the consciousness of the augustness of his being, and the mighty destiny before and awaiting its development, can not fail in this transition period, when you are passing from old theological theories and religious systems into something better, higher, holier, to subserve great and lasting good. In this transition process the great effort is to be made to direct the great body of advancing minds into the right channels, for in many cases the tendency is found to be toward the cold barrenness of materialism.

The question that is to confront you in the future is not in regard to creeds and dogmas, for they are passing away, but whether these few fleeting years of physically embodied life is the all of your being, whether death is the setting forever of the bright star of our being in the night and gloom of ended existence, or whether there is for man a glorious life of endless progress beyond the life and transitory scenes of physical embodiment.

July 14—With this my labors for the present end. The effort has been more irksome than you may conceive. The difficulties attending the act of communicating are more numerous and troublesome than the world would allow if they were fully explained. But we have done the best we could.

To you, Mr. Helleberg, I return my thanks and the thanks of those co-operating with me, for the patience, earnestness and honesty which have characterized your association with us in this work. Our blessings rest upon you, and be assured that your greatest reward will be in the happy land which your aged footsteps are nearing. We shall shield and bless you here, and crown you in the land of immortal beatitudes.

We would be ungrateful beyond measure not to speak in acknowledgment of the virtues and noble qualities of the medium, through whose superbly developed medial powers we have been enabled to speak to the world. In consequence of our frequent contact with her noble and pure soul our first admiration for her has grown into the deepest, truest and holiest affection. Heaven bless her in all her ways and walks. Her noble band of spirits, tireless, indefatigable and upright, have rendered us vast assistance, without which we could not have succeeded in the slightest degree. They are capable, true and honest, and able to guard and protect their instrument, before whom is a great future career of usefulness, and she may confidently trust them in all things.

To those who may read my feeble lines I bespeak that charity you would like extended to you. Judge not harshly, but with generous impulse. You are in the realm of crude materiality, in the tenement of flesh, influenced more or less by many disadvantageous surroundings, which are not spiritually inspiring or elevating, but by and by you will survive and pass beyond them. Let me entreat you to study and learn of the great law of progression, which we have constantly endeavored to keep before you. In that law and its manifold manifestations reside all wisdom, love and truth. It is that law that assures your future greatness and happiness, and will work out for you a destiny, the grandeur and glory of which you can but faintly comprehend and know. You can not die. You must live forever. You can not retrace your steps, nor recede in the development of your being; neither can you stand still. Therefore you must move forward, onward and upward, forever and forever.

— FREDRIKA EHRENBORG

BIBLIOGRAPHY

All selections featured within these pages were pulled from the list of books and publications below. This is only a small sampling of the many alleged spirit writings recorded by mediums from the mid nineteenth century to the early twentieth century.

"A Chat with Mark Twain." *Azoth*, October 1919, Vol. 5, No 4.

"A Grand Poem." *The Daily Phoenix*, October 16, 1872.

Barker, Elsa. *Letters from a Living Dead Man*. New York: E. P. Dutton & Company, 1920.

Burr, William H. *Photographic Copies of Written Messages from the Spirit World*. Rochester: The Avondale Press, 1918.

Doyle, Sir Arthur Conan. *The History of Spiritualism, Vol. 1*. London: Cassell and Company, Ltd., 1926.

Doyle, Sir Arthur Conan. *Pheneas Speaks: Direct Spirit Communications in the Family Circle*. The Psychic Press and Bookshop, 1927.

The Experiences and Opinions of George Washington from Spirit Life. San Francisco, 1878.

Francis, J. R. *The Encyclopaedia of Death and Life in the Spirit-World*. Chicago: The Progressive Thinker Publishing House, 1903.

Grierson, Francis. *Psycho-Phone Messages*. Los Angeles: Austin Publishing Company, 1921.

Helleberg, C. G. *A Book Written by the Spirits of the So-Called Dead*. Cincinnati, 1883.

Horn, Henry J. *Strange Visitors*. New York: Carleton, 1869.

Horn, S. G. *The Next World Interviewed*. Chicago: The Progressive Thinker Publishing House, 1896.

Jap Herron: A Novel Written From the Ouija Board. New York: Mitchell Kennerley, 1917.

Kiddle, Henry. *Spiritual Communications*. New York: The Authors' Publishing Company, 1879.

"Latest Works of Fiction." *New York Times*, September 9, 1917.

Owen, J. J. *Psychography: Marvelous Manifestations of Psychic Power Given Through the Mediumship of Fred P. Evans*. San Francisco: The Hicks-Judd Co., 1893.

Phifer, Lincoln. *Hamlet in Heaven*. Girard, Kansas: Self-published, 1916.

Post, Isaac. *Voices from the Spirit-World*. Rochester: Charles H. McDonell, 1852.

Rafferty, Fred. *Spirit World and Spirit Life*. Los Angeles: J. F. Rowny Press, 1922.

The Spiritual Herald: A Record of Spirit Manifestations. Vol. 1, No. 6, July 1856.

Stead, William. *After Death, or Letters from Julia*. Chicago: The Progressive Thinker Publishing House, 1910.

Stead, Estelle and Pardoe Woodman. *The Blue Island: Experiences of a New Arrival Beyond the Veil*. London: Hutchinson & Co., 1922.

Thornton, Gregory. *Sonnets of Shakespeare's Ghost*. Angus & Robertson, 1920.

Underwood, Sara A. *Automatic or Spirit Writing, With Other Psychic Experiences*. Chicago: Thomas G. Newman, 1896.

ALSO FROM CURIOUS PUBLICATIONS

The Embalmed Head of Oliver Cromwell: A Memoir
by Marc Hartzman

Psycho-Phone Messages
by Francis Grierson

Spectropia, or Surprising Spectral Illusions Showing Ghosts Everywhere
by J. H. Brown

Spirit Slate Writing and Kindred Phenomena
by William E. Robinson

The Sight of Hell
by Rev. John Furniss

How to Speak With the Dead: A Practical Handbook
by Sciens

curiouspublications.com

www.ingramcontent.com/pod-product-compliance
Lightning Source LLC
Chambersburg PA
CBHW030438300426
44112CB00009B/1058